FOUL DEEDS & SUSPICIOUS DEATHS
IN THE
ISLE OF WIGHT

TRUE CRIME FROM WHARNCLIFFE
Foul Deeds and Suspicious Deaths Series

Barking, Dagenham & Chadwell Heath
Barnet, Finchley and Hendon
Barnsley
Bath
Bedford
Birmingham
Black Country
Blackburn and Hyndburn
Bolton
Bradford
Brighton
Bristol
Cambridge
Carlisle
Chesterfield
Colchester
Cotswolds, The
Coventry
Croydon
Derby
Dublin
Durham
Ealing
Fens, In and Around
Folkstone and Dover
Grimsby
Guernsey
Guildford
Halifax
Hampstead, Holborn and St Pancras
Huddersfield
Hull

Jersey
Leeds
Leicester
Lewisham and Deptford
Liverpool
London's East End
London's West End
Manchester
Mansfield
More Foul Deeds Birmingham
More Foul Deeds Chesterfield
More Foul Deeds Wakefield
Newcastle
Newport
Norfolk
Northampton
Nottingham
Oxfordshire
Pontefract and Castleford
Portsmouth
Rotherham
Scunthorpe
Shrewsbury and Around Shropshire
Southampton
Southend-on-Sea
Staffordshire and The Potteries
Stratford and South Warwickshire
Tees
Uxbridge
Warwickshire
Wigan
York

OTHER TRUE CRIME BOOKS FROM WHARNCLIFFE

A-Z of London Murders, The
A-Z of Yorkshire Murders, The
Black Barnsley
Brighton Crime and Vice 1800-2000
Crafty Crooks and Conmen
Durham Executions
Essex Murders
Executions & Hangings in Newcastle
  and Morpeth
Great Hoaxers, Artful Fakers and
  Cheating Charlatans
Norfolk Mayhem and Murder

Norwich Murders
Plot to Kill Lloyd George
Romford Outrage
Strangeways Hanged
Unsolved Murders in Victorian &
  Edwardian London
Unsolved London Murders
Unsolved Norfolk Murders
Unsolved Yorkshire Murders
Warwickshire's Murderous Women
Yorkshire Hangmen
Yorkshire's Murderous Women

Please contact us via any of the methods below for more information or a catalogue
WHARNCLIFFE BOOKS
47 Church Street, Barnsley, South Yorkshire, S70 2AS
Tel: 01226 734555 • 734222 • Fax: 01226 734438
email: enquiries@pen-and-sword.co.uk
website: www.wharncliffebooks.co.uk

Foul Deeds & Suspicious Deaths in the
ISLE OF WIGHT

M J Trow

First Published in Great Britain in 2009 by
Wharncliffe Books
an imprint of
Pen and Sword Books Limited,
47 Church Street, Barnsley,
South Yorkshire. S70 2AS

Copyright © M.J. Trow, 2009

ISBN: 978 184563 088 1

The right of M J Trow to be identified as
author of this work has been asserted by him
in accordance with the Copyright, Designs and Patents Act, 1988.

A CIP catalogue record of this book is available from the
British Library.

Typeset in Plantin and Benguiat by
S L Menzies-Earl

Printed in the UK by the MPG Books Group

Pen & Sword Books Ltd incorporates the imprints of
Pen & Sword Aviation, Pen & Sword Maritime,
Pen & Sword Military, Wharncliffe Local History, Pen & Sword Select,
Pen & Sword Military Classics, Leo Cooper, Remember When, Seaforth Publishing
and Frontline Publishing

For a complete list of Pen & Sword titles please contact:
PEN & SWORD BOOKS LIMITED
47 Church Street, Barnsley, South Yorkshire, S70 2AS, England.
E-mail: enquiries@pen-and-sword.co.uk
Website: www.pen-and-sword.co.uk

Contents

Acknowledgements

My thanks go to the following for their co-operation and spirit of friendliness in the production of this book: the editor and staff of the Isle of Wight *County Press*, the licensees and staff of the *Hare and Hounds* public house, Downend, the licensees and staff of the *Buddle Inn*, Niton, the churchwarden and PCC, Newport Minster, Andrew Ross, Hairdressing, Newport, Just You beauticians, Newport.

I would also like to thank Mrs Debbie Galvin for her help, and above all my good lady wife, Carol Trow, for many hours trekking over the Isle of Wight in all weathers to take the photographs in this book. And finally to my son, Tali, who knows where the bodies are buried!

Chapter 1

Alarums and Incursions

T here is only one line that tells us anything about the Roman invasion of the Isle of Wight. The biographer Suetonius wrote that Vespasian, sweeping along the south coast with the II Legio Augusta, took Vectis (the Island), defeated two warlike tribes (*validissime gentes*) and captured over twenty fortresses (*oppida*). The tribes were probably the Durotriges of what is today Dorset and the Dobunni further east in what would become Hampshire and Sussex. The fortresses are more likely to be hill-top forts on the mainland, but there is at least the possibility of one standing on a hill in the centre of the Island which is now the site of Carisbrooke Castle.

What was Vespasian doing in the Island in the first place? He was part of the Claudian invasion of AD 43 , but that is in itself a misnomer. The Emperor Claudius was hardly the stuff of which soldiers are made and if he was not exactly the limping, stammering idiot of Robert Graves' famous novel, he was certainly no general. He turned up, as Emperors often did, at the very end of the campaign, to claim laurels and wave to crowds - and came nowhere near Vectis.

The hard work was done by Aulus Plautius, who began a systematic attack on the disunited tribes of Britain, using the formidable tactics of

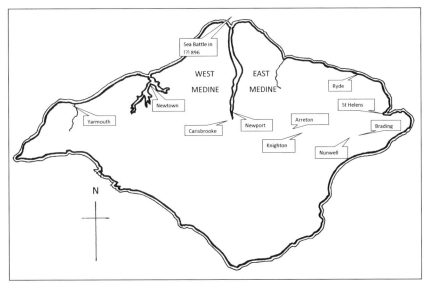

Location map 1. The author

The general who conquered the Isle of Wight – the future emperor Vespasian, from a marble bust. The author

the Roman legions. Worthy opponents like Caratacus were driven back into the forested mountains of Wales and Vespasian, with just a single legion, was taking a huge gamble in his march westward along the south coast.

With his cavalry, his auxiliary units, his legion, siege engines and ballistae, he may have had 10,000 men at his back – but that was probably more than the total number of fighting men in the Isle of Wight.

The fact that Suetonius makes so little of the Roman invasion of the Island and that other writers do not refer to it at all, probably implies that there was little or perhaps no resistance. The rapidly growing *imperium* that was Rome meant that southern regions of Britannia, including the island, had been trading with the eternal city for at least a generation by the time Vespasian arrived. Pre-Claudian coins have been found here and amphorae discovered in marine silt are evidence of a thriving wine import. We know that Celtic leaders in southern Britain like Togodumnos based at Chichester, were only too happy to accept a latinized version of his name and all the panoply of Roman client kingship that went with it.

What has survived from the Roman period of Vectis is a string of villas, eight of which have so far been discovered, implying an ordered, settled, peaceful way of life. Military camps, of the type found at legionary bases from Exeter to the later Hadrian's Wall, do not feature and probably never did. Only at Carisbrooke, at the base of the Norman earthworks thrown up in the 1070s, do we have a section of a stone wall which is probably Roman.

By the early fifth century, as the legions were withdrawn from mainland Britain, the Island's villas began to fall into decline. There is evidence that the wealthy owners abandoned their properties as early as the 390s, perhaps because of Saxon raids on what was a largely defenceless island. The first record of such attacks comes from the Anglo-Saxon Chronicle, a series of four texts produced from the late 9th century which traces a sketchy 'history' of the country from 60 BC. In the year 530, Cerdic and Cynric seized the Isle of Wight and killed a few men at Carisbrook. What does this tell us? First, there was definitely resistance to Saxon incursions. Whereas the Celtic Islanders had a history of trade links with Rome and could see advantages out of a Romano-British society, the wild, flaxen-haired strangers offered nothing but theft and death. The origins of

The church at Brading, perhaps the first Christian settlement in the Isle of Wight. The town itself was a busy port until land reclamation in the late seventeenth century. Carol Trow

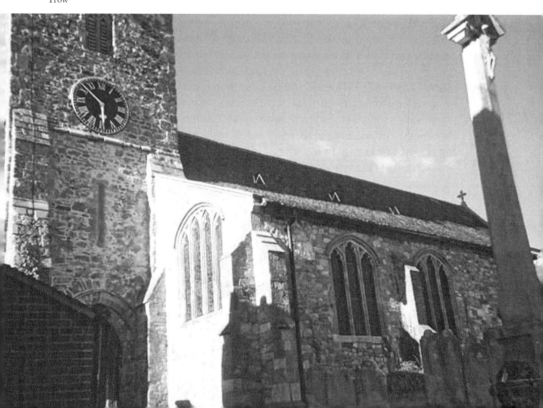

Christianity on the Island are shadowy, but it is probable that religious differences were an issue too – the invaders were pagan, bent on destroying not only the houses of God, like the church at Brading, but the concept of a single deity too. The fact that the Saxon warlords killed men at Carisbrooke implies that the old Celtic/Roman fortress still stood as a focal point of Island defences.

Cerdic was king of the West Saxons and four years after the attack on Carisbrooke gave the Island to his nephews Stuf and Whitgar.

Over a century later, we hear of further depredations. In 661, Wulfhoe, son of Penda of Mercia 'ravaged the Isle of Wight and gave the inhabitants over to Aethelnold, King of Sussex...Eoppa the priest, at Wilfrid's word and that of King Wulfhoe, first among men, brought the people of Wight baptism.'

The Island was in fact a pawn in the bitter hostility between the southern Saxon kingdoms, jockeying for power and the most serious attack came in the 680s under the leadership of Caedwalla, King of Wessex. He was the most brilliant war leader to be linked with the Island since Vespasian and in less than a year had defeated the bands who opposed him in three southern counties. On the Island, Aethelnold was killed and his sons brought before Caedwalla. They were baptized at the point of the sword and then executed. The extent of Caedwalla's onslaught is impossible to measure. We only have the Chronicle record, but the implications are that large numbers of locals fled to the mainland for safety and those who remained became 'wild men in the woods'. The ambiguity of Island faith in this period would not be settled until Caedwalla's successor, Ine (688-726) established a series of laws – the Dooms – which were among the first codifications of English judiciary.

By the late 780s, the English coast had become the target of raids by the Vikings, fierce sea-rovers from Scandinavia who could not resist the soft touches and gold plate of English monasteries. Such was the speed of Viking attacks that a raiding party could strike and be gone before any organised resistance could be set up. Southampton was sacked in 842; Winchester, the capital of what would become England, in 860. Not until the brilliant stand by Alfred would the Vikings be held by treaty in their North Eastern Danelaw and even then the peace was precarious. In 896 for example, 'six ships came to the Isle of Wight and did much evil there'... It is not absolutely clear where the naval engagement took place, but if 'the river's mouth in the open sea' refers to the Medina, then a major confrontation which is well chronicled took place just off the Island. The aged Alfred sent nine new warships, of the long-boat design, to tackle the Viking pirates and sunk two of their ships. The third one got away, but only five of its crew survived. Viking sea-battles were fought as on land, with the ships locked together with grappling hooks and ropes as one crew boarded the enemy ship and hacked at their opponents on the deck. The ebbing tide stranded both sides' ships and not until it turned could the Vikings escape. The Anglo-Saxon Chronicle records the dead – 'there were killed Lucumen the king's reeve [steward], Wulfhead the Frisian, Aebbe the Frisian, Aethelhue the Frisian, Athelferth of the king's household and in all, Frisians and English, sixty two and one hundred and twenty of the Danes'. The implication is that this was not a battle fought by Islanders, the casualties referring to Alfred's professionals from Winchester or Frisian allies/mercenaries.

Viking depredations came again to the Island early in the eleventh century. The long-reigning Aethelred II must have had a certain ability to have lasted as long as he did, but he earned the nickname 'Unraed' – badly advised – and he was certainly no match for Sweyn Forkbeard and his son Cnut who began a series of raids which culminated in full-blown conquest by 1016. Much of the fighting took place in the north and east, but the raiders used the Island as a handy springboard for attacks as far inland as Waltham in Sussex and even struck as far west as Exeter. We have no idea where precisely the invaders stayed and the Anglo-Saxon Chronicle's entry for 1006 is ambiguous. It implies that Aethelred's army stayed in the field all Autumn (always unpopular because of the vital need to gather in the harvest) but that as soon as they disbanded, the Vikings arrived 'after Martinmas [November] on the Island' and 'obtained everywhere there whatever they needed' (one assumes, by force). Once there, they struck out across Hampshire and Berkshire sacking villages and lighting beacons to mark the path of their destruction.

The Island's role in the complex manoeuvrings of 1066 is vague. Three men laid claim that year to the crown of England, vacated by the death of Edward the Confessor in January. A fourth, Tostig, the exiled brother of the contender Harold Godwinson, Earl of Wessex, came, according to the Chronicle 'across the sea into the Isle of Wight, with as many household troops as he could gather and was given money and provisions'. However, Harold's plans seem to have thwarted him. He knew that William of Normandy was mounting an invasion and itched to beat him at sea where his deadly cavalry, an innovation on European battlefields at the time, would be useless. To that end, Godwinson's massive fleet of perhaps 100 ships prowled the Solent and Tostig fled north, to die in battle with Harold and the Viking king Hardrada at Stamford Bridge near York in September.

There are no records of the subsequent Norman arrival on the Island. The battle near Senlac was won on 14 October and William crowned at Westminster on Christmas Day. It would probably have been well into the following year when William Fitz Osbern, Constable of Normandy, took over what was probably a Saxon hill fort at Carisbrooke and set about building a wooden motte-and-bailey castle to subdue the populace. From its high keep, the castle's defenders could see the Solent in two places, had a clear view up the river Medina to the north coast and any attacking army could take half a day to reach Carisbrooke from their first being sighted. It had two separate wells to provide water and crops and livestock could be driven quickly behind the oak palisades from the villages of Carisbrooke and Shide in the event of a siege. The whole castle keep, curtain wall and towers, was built of stone by 1136.

In that year, national politics caused the Island problems when the country split into factions under the rival royal claimants, Stephen and Matilda, both declaring their right to wear the crown of Henry I. The lords of the Island were now the de Redvers family, Richard de Redvers having been granted the title by the king. In the internecine nine years that followed Henry's death, the great feudal lords had to make a choice – Matilda, Henry's daughter or Stephen, his nephew. Perhaps unusually in a patristic society, Baldwin de Redvers threw in his lot with Matilda, but was beaten by Stephen at Exeter. He retreated to Carisbrooke and a siege took place. There is virtually no record of this, but it seems likely that the long dry summer of 1136 caused the castle's well to dry up and de Redvers surrendered. Any marauding army like Stephen's would not have thought twice about commandeering any provisions they saw fit and anyone opposing them would have risked death. None of this, however, is recorded.

If the Island escaped relatively lightly in times of civil war (there is no hint of trouble during the fifteenth-century Wars of the Roses, for example) it was often a target in international politics. Precautions against French attacks continued throughout the period. In 1295 the total cost of the Island's defences, partly borne by the Church, was an astonishing £467 18s 2d. Professional *balistarii* (crossbowmen) were brought from London to provide a nucleus of military talent should the inevitable happen. The outbreak of the Hundred Years War which saw Edward III lay claim to the French throne led to sporadic raids on the Island. It also meant that the Island had to provide thirteen ships and 222 mariners as part of the war effort. The fourteenth century is seen as 'the hurling time' when a protracted war, the scourge of bubonic plague and the outbreak of the Peasants' Revolt were regarded by contemporaries as the wrath of God or the work of the devil. Perhaps 40% of the Island's population perished between 1349 and 1352; among the great landowners, two of the Oglander family from Nunwell. Nine years earlier, a French raiding party hit St Helens and Theobald Russell, who led the defence, died from his wounds in his home at Knighton. There was a royal ban on locals leaving the Island and young men were expected to practise weekly with that most deadly of English 'secret' weapons, the longbow. All able-bodied men between fifteen and sixty were included and from 1321 there had been regular inspections of the local levy and their weapons.

The next attack was on 21 August 1377. The early phases of the war in France had seen spectacular English victories at battles like Crecy and Poitiers but by now the tide was beginning to turn. The country's best generals, Edward III and his son, the Black Prince, were both dead and the new king was the ten year old Richard II. It was a perfect time for a French *chevauchee* (raid) and they struck hard. Landing somewhere on the north coast, possibly at La Rie (Ryde) the army marched as far inland as Arreton. Their principle targets, in search of booty, were the three major towns of Francheville, Yarmouth and Newport. The thirteen beacons in Eastmedine and the sixteen west of the river were no doubt lit to warn Islanders of the raiders' advance.

Today, all that is left of Francheville (free town) is the bird sanctuary of Newtown. Its harbour was already silting up by the 1370s, but its relative decline did not save it from total destruction. A later town hall and a scattering of houses made from medieval stone are all that remain. Under the fields, the grid pattern of the streets – Gold Street and Silver Street are prominent – is still clear. Newport was so badly burned that the town

Silver Street, one of the main thoroughfares in Frenchville, destroyed by the French raid of 1377. Today called Newtown, it is a bird sanctuary and nature trail. Carol Trow

Peter de Heynoe, Lord of Stenbury, takes aim with his strongbow. The author

was said to be uninhabitable for nearly two years. The priory of St Cross and its outlying mills were burned along the Medina and then the army came to Carisbrooke.

The castle's far-sighted defenders had moved with the times and the walls had wooden brattices along their lengths to add to the formidable defences. The gatehouse had been extended to include a drawbridge, two, perhaps three portcullises and gigantic drum towers with loops for crossbows. It was through one of these, by tradition in the west curtain wall, that Peter de Heynoe, a garrison commander who was lord of Stenbury, is said to have fired his silver bow that killed the French commander. He was one of forty full-time crossbowmen permanently on standby at the castle.

According to an eighteenth-century account Carisbrooke's garrison was composed of nine companies of militia, which included reinforcements from Southampton and London. If that was so, then the castle must have been crammed to bursting point, what with trembling civilians and their livestock. The overall commander was Sir Hugh Tyrril who seems to have led a sortie against the besieging army, ambushing them in a narrow lane, now called Deadman's and burying the dead under a tumulus called, mockingly, Noddies Hill (today, Nodehill is a part of Newport).

The French must now have faced a dilemma. If de Heynoe had killed their commander, the next most senior nobleman had to weigh up the pros and cons. Carisbrooke could hold out for months with its double well and its provisions and October's weather would make a siege that dragged on into winter uncomfortable under canvas. We know from an inventory of 1359 that stores included salt, hemp, horsehair, wheat, barley, peas, bacon, iron, hay, sea-coal, wine, honey, wax, dog-fish skins, crossbows and longbows. And how long would it be before reinforcements were sent from the mainland and the besieging army itself besieged? In the end, the Islanders agreed to pay 1000 marks not to have their homes burned and not to resist if the French returned within one year.

Another attack occurred in 1404 and this time the Island's response was more robust. The French boasted that they would spend Christmas here, but were suddenly ambushed while driving cattle to their ships. Not only did they lose their plunder, but several of their men too.

The last sortie by the French took place soon afterwards and seems to have been no more than a scratch party of *jacquerie*, the mercenaries who had made life intolerable across France, trying their luck. The information comes from the Elizabethan antiquary John Stowe who claimed that a large fleet arrived demanding a subsidy in the name of King Richard and his second wife, Queen Isabella of Valois. If this 'invasion' happened in 1404, Richard had been dead for five years by then and Isabella had long since returned to France. The Islanders pointed all this out, gave the French six hours to rest from their Channel crossing (which seems extraordinarily chivalrous) then offered to meet them in the field. The French declined. So, after centuries of invasion and an unknown loss of life, the Islands 'Alarums and Incursions' ended in pure farce.

Chapter 2

Medieval Murder

E videnced of murder in the Island during the Middle Ages comes to us directly from one source only – the coroner's court proceedings from July 1377 to Michaelmas (Autumn) 1392. It lists forty-two cases and it would be fascinating to compare these years with earlier periods. This was, after all, the 'hurling time' of the Hundred Years' War and the Peasants' Revolt; was this a worse time than any other as far as Island serious crime was concerned?

Until her death in 1293, the redoubtable Isabella de Fortibus was the Lady of the Wight and ruled the place as her private domain from Carisbrooke Castle. Widowed at twenty-three, the murder of her brother Baldwin (de Redvers) two years later catapulted her into the arena of male-dominated politics. For most of her rule, she was in constant litigation with abbeys and other landholders over rights and was regularly involved in other legal wrangles. She also acted as coroner, which was usually a role reserved for the king's appointee, and even after Edward I acquired the Island from Isabella on her deathbed, the Governor of the Island continued to act as coroner in his own right, as well as bailiff and sheriff.

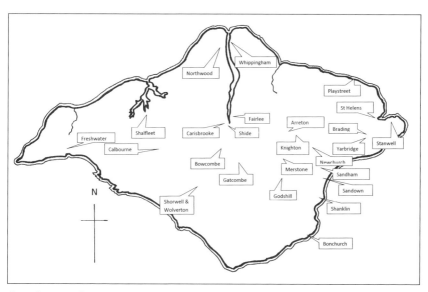

Location map 2. The author

in·in·insula·uect

Isabella de Fortibus was the last independent ruler of the Isle of Wight. From a stone carving in Christchurch, Hampshire. The author

One or two cases emerge from just before Isabella's reign from the assize court in Southampton to which Island cases were sent at the time. In 1255, brothers Richard and Thomas le Noreis entered a not guilty plea of the murder of Peter de Wyppingeham. Their argument was that the supposed victim was alive and well and living overseas, so that there was no case to answer. Infuriatingly, there is no record of the outcome of the case, but it must have turned on the issue of *corpus delicti*, the existence of an actual body to prove murder, which serial killer John George Haigh believed was still in operation in 1949 when he was charged with the murder of Olivia Durand-Deacon.

At the same assize in Southampton, William Bold stood accused of the murder of Ivo Urry. Again, the result is not recorded, but Bold had been arrested in the Island and taken to Carisbrooke castle from which he had escaped. Perhaps pursued by the mob under the law of hue and cry, Bold ran to Godshill church where he claimed right of sanctuary. Under medieval law, he could remain safe on church property for forty days. After that, presumably, the waiting law took its course and Bold found himself on his way to Southampton.

The Coroner's Roll from the fourteenth century is almost as disappointing as the Southampton Assize in terms of hard fact. The job of the coroner was to call a jury, usually of twelve men, but this could vary, to ascertain the cause in any case of sudden death. Such juries were always local and local knowledge of the deceased might be useful. Usually the only witness called was the 'first-finder' of the corpse and then the jury and coroner had to decide the cause of death and the *deodand*, the value of the murder weapon (if murder it was) and the worth of the supposed culprit. This was the sole concern of the coroner – subsequent trials of suspects are not recorded, so we have no idea how the various cases turned out.

The jurymen came from two clusters of parishes – 'Brerdyng, Sandham, Knyghtone and Seynthelyn' (Brading, Sandham, Knighton and Shanklin) or 'Carysbrooke, Shyde, Northwodde, Fayrle' (Carisbrooke, Shide, Northwood [Cowes] and Fairlee [Newport]). Of the forty-three cases listed, nine involved drowning, fifteen death by misadventure and eighteen designated 'murder'.

In the drowning cases, four were toddlers who fell into wells and judging by the dates of the courts (the coroner usually called his juries the day after the body was found) they were the unwarranted result of little children playing in the summer when their parents were busy with the harvest. So John the Hulle, aged one-and-a-half, drowned in July 1377. Three years later, another John, the two-and-a-half-year-old son of John Favell was found floating at Stanwell, Bembridge by his distraught

Medieval sanctuary - those who reached this doorway of the church at Godshill were safe from secular laws, at least in theory. C M Trow

mother. Two-year-old Helen Couherd was found by her mother Julia at Langbridge in the same year and Julian Breketo, also two, was found by Alice Summers, probably a neighbour.

Adult drownings are better chronicled. Richard Croucher went to St Helens harbour on the Monday after St James (25 July) 1380 to 'wash and bathe in the sea'. His legs gave way and he drowned. It was weeks after his death in the salt-water river at Croklyd, Shalfleet that William Rouclie was found by his mother, Christina. Florence Smythe was found face down in the river at Newchurch by Joan Caphill. And John Tanner went under for the last time when a sudden gust of wind overturned his fishing boat in Newport harbour, opposite Dodnor Creek in February 1383.

One of the drownings was recorded as a suicide. This was rare in the Middle Ages as it was regarded as a mortal sin; not only did a man's soul wander for ever in purgatory, but the corpse could not be buried in consecrated ground and the deceased's goods were forfeit to the crown. We have no idea why Isabella, the wife of William Baas left her house near midnight on Sunday 12 December 1388 but she walked to the Yar Bridge and threw herself *'ex mera voluntate'* (of her own will) into the icy waters.

A number of the sudden deaths recorded in the Coroner's Roll are work-related accidents. Richard Warder was dragged to death by a bolting colt in June 1390 at Calbourne. Since the cause of death was the animal, it (as the instrument of decease) was the *deodand*, valued at ten shillings. Adam Porter fell off the roof of St Thomas's church in Newport soon after Palm Sunday in 1386 and broke his neck. Edward Dryver had his head crushed to a pulp when his cart and horses rolled over him after a fall. This was in Playstrete, a stretch of open country to the south-west of Ryde and the deodand (horse and cart) was 26s 8d. Another horse was involved the following year when Thomas Evede tried to prevent his black animal and another fighting in Pyle Street, Newport. The rearing animal kicked him fatally in the head.

Two children were scalded to death in the same year, 1390. Two-and-a-half-year-old William Wray and rather younger John Elof of Bonchurch paid the price of the open fires of the time. In each case the value of the guilty pan was 4d.

In a case which has curious echoes in the health and safety/litigation mentality of today, teenager Richard Cordey was killed at Shepstret, Arreton, while trying to lift a fallen oak tree with a group of friends. Since the land (and tree) belonged to Quarr Abbey, the monks were responsible for the *deodand* value of 8d.

Two of the strangest cases, classed as accidents by the historian Dom Hockey in 1982, really belong to other categories. Geoffrey Waryn of Whitwell was found dead in the house of John Clare in Newport. The man was ill with what he assumed was a hernia, but was in all probability a testicular hydrocoele which would have caused painful swelling in the groin. He was operated on by Gerard Gros using a razor and died as a result. It is not at all clear what qualifications, if any, Gros had. Medicine in the fourteenth century was still based on the pseudo-science of the Greek doctor Galen, 1200 years earlier, which believed that all bodily malfunctions were the result of an imbalance of the four humours. Surgery, without anaesthetic, antiseptics or any knowledge of bacteria was hugely risky and deaths must have been frequent. Even so, this is the only recorded instance in fifteen years. The razor was worth 4d and Gros's goods, a dagger and cloak, 4 shillings.

In what was clearly a case of self-defence, Thomas Compton killed William Bole in a 'war-game' situation that got out of hand. This was March 1380, only three years after the latest French invasion and the men of the Wight were expected to practise regularly in case of a repetition of that. The records do not tell us why, but Bole attacked Compton with a quarter-staff. In defence, Compton stabbed him with his sword. The inquest was held at Southtowne (part of Freshwater) and Bole's worldly goods were assessed at 8 shillings; his sword was worth 6d.

Of the eighteen murder cases that took place between 1377 and 1392, all of them were committed by men and almost all involved knives. Today we are obsessed with knife crime as though it is something new, pernicious and symptomatic of the twenty-first-century breakdown of society. This medieval evidence, which is no doubt replicated all over the country, shows that nothing could be further from the truth. In one case only is the murder weapon an expensive one. Described as a 'Gascoynge knife' it was used to kill John Grontale in a fight at Fennycombe (Venniscombe) late in November of 1377. This was almost certainly a baselard or poignard, the kind of gilt or silver hilted, double-edged dagger carried by knights; its *deodand* value was 4 shillings. In all other cases, the murder weapons were 'thwittles' (spellings vary) which are the cheap, badly-produced knives carried by all labourers.

The Grontale case is the first recorded in the Coroner's Roll. His killer, acting in self-defence, was John Alwyn and Grontale seems to have fallen

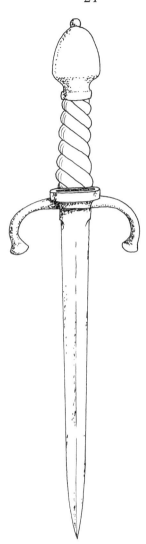

A Gascoigne knife, an expensive medieval dagger. The fourteenth-century Coroner's Roll tells us that the most common murder weapon was a cheap version of this one. The author

on the knife in the course of a struggle which he started. All the records date the crime, or at least the inquest, by the church calendar. So, on the Saturday before the Exaltation of the Cross (14 September 1378) Walter Tauntone battered Richard Matesford over the head with a shovel on the road between Huffingford and Merston. The body was found by Roger Bodenor and by the time the inquest was held on 21 September, Tauntone had absconded.

There must have been a long-standing set of differences between Walter Peddar and John Hawkyn because on the Tuesday before Ascension 1379, he dashed out of his house at Kern, Brading and hit Hawkyn twice, although with what weapon is not recorded. Hawkyn fought back, stabbing Peddar in the arm to the depth of four inches. He presumably died from loss of blood. Hawkyn's goods were valued at ten shillings.

A very determined attack was recorded on the Monday before Whit Monday, 1381. At a point on the road between Newchurch and Polesdown, John Saverage attacked Benesius Athersam, first with a quarter staff and then with a dagger in the left side. The inquest at Whitchurch found that Saverage had no goods and his knife was worth 4d.

Another feud was resolved early in January 1383. John Underwode and Robert Gibberd had exchanged insults on the Sunday before 6 January, perhaps on their way to or from church in Sandown and a week later, Underwode's rage boiled over and he attacked Gilberd, hitting him twice with an unrecorded weapon. Gilberd retaliated, almost certainly with a knife and Underwode died. There were no *deodand* goods involved and the knife was valued at 2d.

A rather dubious coroner's verdict was delivered at the end of June 1383 when the case of Philip Bochere's murder was recorded. The man had been stabbed in the back by William Anstey and, as usual, no motive is given. Anstey's knife had the same value as his worldly goods – 12d – but in this case, the vill [manor] of Bowcombe was held to be responsible; there is no explanation given for this.

Shortly after Christmas 1385, more resentment boiled over in the 'king's' town of Brading when Nicholas Gentleyman went to neighbour John Tyton's house and knocked him down, striking him on the arm. Tyton fought back with his knife and Gentleyman died in the struggle, wounded in the left side. Tyton fled to the sanctuary of Brading church and stayed there for two days. On the Monday following the fight, he agreed to meet the coroner and his men at the church gate. Still technically untouchable by virtue of standing on holy ground, he admitted his guilt but was allowed to 'abjure the realm', in other words leave the country. This is a rare example of the recording of at least a partial 'result' and only because all such exiles had to be noted. Tyton left via the port of St Helens.

Days before the Gentleyman killing, Walter Ware stabbed John Clarke to the depth of five inches in a tavern at Shorwell. What is interesting about this murder is the light it sheds on the drinking habits of the time; 21 December 1385 was a Sunday and the pubs were open!

Alcohol was again involved in January 1388. A fight broke out in Showesflete, (Shofflet in Whippingham), between Nicholas Baker and Richard Drynkwater. John Carter, who is recorded as a servant of Newport, tried to break it up and was rewarded with Baker breaking a beer bottle over his head. Carter hit back with a staff and killed him. As befitted his status, he had no goods.

Whereas many of the murders in the Coroner's Rolls were fights that turned fatal, the attack on Richard Brykeville on the road between Yarbridge and Wolverton was probably a mugging that went wrong. It happened on 15 August 1389 when Robert Cornamton and John Nave lay in wait for him. It is not clear whether this was a personal attack or whether the pair were professional robbers. By the late fourteenth century, Parkhurst Forest had been much reduced in size because of farming and the need for timber for building, so gangs of the Robin Hood/Sherwood type are unlikely. That said, some parts of the Island are remote and desolate even today and this would have been even more true in the past.

The last two entries in the Roll refer to priests. Their position was always controversial in terms of law because in effect they served two masters. As ordained clergy, they owed allegiance to the Pope and had their own canonical courts, which were seen as unusually lenient in terms of punishment. As Englishmen, they were of course also subjects of the king, but were exempt from civil legislation and as such, something of a law unto themselves. Interestingly, this period – the 1380s – is the decade in which Geoffrey Chaucer wrote his parody *The Canterbury Tales* which satirizes the society in which he lived. Of the eight church pilgrims in the stories, only one, the town parson, is a good man; all the others have long ago broken any vows they ever took.

On the Island however, in the two cases listed, the priests were victims. No motive is given for the attack which took place on All Saints' Day 1389. William Westerfield was a chaplain, that is a priest without a living and he was stabbed in the stomach by Robert Acle at Shide field between Gatcombe and Newport. Acle fled and was presumably not caught, although without further information, we cannot know why his name was 'in the frame' in the first place.

The last entry is the oddest in that two inquests were held on the same day, presumably because information came to light after the first one was over. In the earlier hearing, Edward Alderford, the rector of

Punishment past - the whipping post and stocks are now museum exhibits in the King's Town of Brading. CM Trow

Whippingham, was accused of hacking William Wonforton, servant of the superior (abbot) of Barton oratory, twice with a sword. The incident happened at the north end of Fairlee on Whit Monday 1391. The story went that William Alderford, the rector's brother and a friend, Michael Pycard, had aided and abetted. Bearing in mind that churchmen were supposed to have taken a vow of poverty, the list of Alderford's goods is astonishing (but would not have surprised Chaucer). He owned two horses and saddles worth 16 shillings, lambs worth 26s 8d, a pair of sheets valued at 4 shillings and two swords worth 16d. Again, we are entitled to ask why a man of God, pledged to turning the other cheek, should have owned swords at all. The oddest items are the two 'trussyncoffres', worth two shillings; these were probably linen chests. Alderford fled, taking everything but the lambs with him. Pycard and the rector's brother fled with him.

The second inquest of the day cast a different light on the incident. It was revealed that Michael Pycard was also a servant of the superior of Barton and that William Wonforton had hit him first. The rector appeared and broke up the fight by grabbing Wonforton's tunic. Wonforton pulled a knife and slashed the rector in the face and arm. William Alderford intervened at this point and was also knocked down. The jurors of the second inquest decided that in the fracas that followed, Michael Pycard was the real killer, having pole-axed Wonforton with a quarter staff which caught him above the right ear. As always, the fate of the participants is unknown.

Annoyingly incomplete though the Coroner's Roll is, the cases do tell a story. By comparison with today, the murder rate is extraordinarily high, averaging over the period at almost two a year in an area whose population is unlikely to have exceeded four thousand. Assuming that only half that number was male, we have an alarming situation making today's knife-related deaths quite ordinary. In the first half of 2008, such murders in London give us a figure of 0.00044% of the population. In the late fourteenth century in the Isle of Wight, the figure is nearer 0.022% of the population, two hundred times greater. There are no recorded instances of female crime at all, although of course other records, like those of the leet or manor courts, would have to be taken into account to give us an overall picture. Sadly, such details have not survived.

Chapter 3

The Sea Beggars

By definition, the Isle of Wight has always been heavily reliant on the sea. Legally, it provided fish and a means of transportation. Illegally, it was a pirate's paradise.

Long before the seventeenth century created the buccaneer, capitalized on in later generations by Gilbert and Sullivan and Hollywood, everybody from the lords of the Island to the humblest fishermen proceeded to help themselves to floating goods.

Officially the 'wreck of the sea' belonged to the king. Until the 1290s, private landowners culminating with Isabella de Fortibus claimed it and split the proceeds fifty-fifty between themselves and the Island's gentry. Distinction was made between *flotsam* (floating debris which may be cargo from ships or wrecked ships themselves) and *jetsam* (debris which was deliberately thrown overboard by a merchant crew, usually desperate to keep their vessel afloat in treacherous weather).

A statute of 1324 stated that a ship owner could recover all his goods from a lost or stolen ship if he was physically able to do so within three months. After a year and a day, such goods were forfeit to the crown. This law stood until 1712.

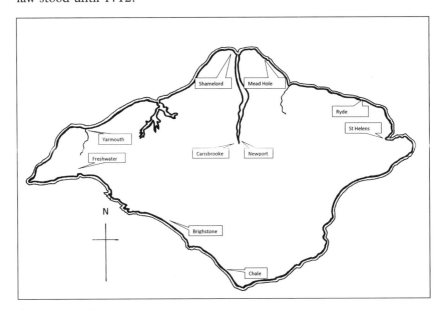

Location map 3. The author

One of the most pernicious misuses of the sea was wrecking, when ships, usually at night and in rough seas, were lured onto the rocks by lanterns offering a safe harbour. There are no known examples of this in the Island but in 1224, Peter des Roches, the Bishop of Winchester (in whose See the Island fell) ordered excommunication for anyone found guilty. It was proclaimed in all Island churches three times a year.

Fourteenth century records, almost all from the Assize of Southampton, catalogue a number of cases of disputes between shipowners and sea-beggars who decided to help themselves to somebody else's property. On 22 April 1313, the *Blessed Mary* out of Bayonne was wrecked on the dangerous rocks below Chale. One hundred and seventy four barrels of white wine were taken from the beach and probably by the time the owners had appealed to king Edward II for redress, it had all been recycled through the population!

In June of the same year, a gang of sea-beggars appeared (eventually) in the Southampton court, led by a man who might be called the Island's first organized criminal – Walter de Godeton – whose name appears more than once in this respect. He, Richard de Hogheton, John Beysam and Ralph de Wolverton at first denied being at Chale at all, but when Beysam cracked and confessed to taking one barrel, the others realized the game was up. De Hogheton took two casks, de Wolverton one. Godeton admitted to obtaining fifty-three barrels and a pipe of wine, but said he bought all this legally from the crew. All three were found guilty, de Godeton losing half his land to provide compensation. Beysam, with no status of his own, stayed in gaol, either in Southampton or Winchester.

Seven years later, another gang should have appeared at the Assize and failed to turn up. The *St Mary* out of Santander was wrecked off Yarmouth, but unlike the Chale incident, there was no consensual bartering with the crew; the goods were taken by force. Again, we have the names of the accused: Geoffrey Snoddone, William Foket, Roger Faber, William de Glot, Robert Atte Brigge, William Sebode, John Atte Wode, William Alfricham and John le Medemowere – but since none of these went to court, no result was obtained. Medieval law said that if a man failed to appear in court four times, he was officially outlawed and his goods seized.

In the next decade, a wreck occurred which proved that bad news travelled surprisingly fast in the Middle Ages and that sea-beggaring was a popular bandwagon. In a summer storm off the Island's south coast, the Portuguese owned *Jesus Christ* was wrecked off Brighstone. All the crew escaped, but the cargo was carted away by up to forty-five men who came from as far afield as Christchurch, Lymington, Milford and Portsmouth. Prominent among Islanders was Walter de Godeton, who is either the same opportunist we have met before or his son.

Stealing from wrecks was one thing; actual piracy and the 'arrest of shipping' another. In 1231 Osbert Perceheys was sailing from Nantes with a cargo of lampreys (eels) which were a popular food at the time. When the weather turned, he put his ship into Freshwater for shelter and his entire cargo disappeared.

An even more brazen incident happened in the early summer of 1292 when five English ships (it is not known how many Islanders were on board) attacked a single Gascon vessel off the Island. Brought to court, the captains swore they believed the ship was Spanish and that, because of international relations at the time, this was simply an act of war. Ironically, the ship was herself a pirate, attacking Flemish and Lombard vessels at sea.

On 16 May 1354, Edward III ordered that the goods of Bartholomew de Camilla be returned to him. *The Seint Michel* out of Dieppe had been carrying hides and fleeces from Lisbon and Seville and was captured in the Solent and towed into Yarmouth harbour. The case was handled by John de Kingeston, bailiff of the Island who, eighteen years earlier, had organized what resistance he could when the French invaded. The trial, held at Yarmouth on the Friday after Ascension Day, decided that the main culprit was John Saleman of Rye, though whether this is Rye is Sussex or La Rie (Ryde) in the Isle of Wight, is unclear.

Mistakes occasionally happened in an age when names were so similar and the wheels of justice ground so slowly. Master John Breton of Nicholas le Hosteller's ship out of Southampton was driven to seek shelter in St Helens harbour and was promptly arrested as an alien. This was October 1368 and England was at war with both France and Spain. Breton was probably trying his luck when he claimed to be an honest fish trader *and* on a special mission from Sir John Chandos, one of the principal English commanders in France. Either way, Breton was in the clear and had to be released.

Rather as today when courts sometimes hand out ludicrously light sentences, the notorious Poole-based pirate Henry (Arry) Paye got off lightly in November 1403 when he merely had to make restitution to a Spanish ship he attacked off the Island the previous month. He had personally killed a crewman and set the owner, John de Garostica, adrift in an open boat in the Channel!

The Island was also a useful hiding place for sea-robbers who struck elsewhere. The *Christoph*, a Breton ship, had its valuable cargo of corn, sheepskins and linen stashed here in 1433. Eight years later, we have the name of the Island's first 'fence' (receiver of stolen goods) when John White of Newport bought a cargo of salt and wine taken from Breton ships by the Cornish pirate Hawkyn de Hode.

Governor, Admiral and friend of pirates - the tomb of Sir Edward Horsey in the Minster Church of St Thomas in Newport. Carol Trow

The age of privateers belongs to the sixteenth century. The increasingly strained relations between England and Spain after the accession of Elizabeth led to a 'cold war' that eventually became a hot one. English sailors were encouraged, via the Admiralty, to take on the silver-laden Spanish convoys coming home from the Americas and to share their loot with the Queen's government. Much of this was strictly 'off the record' and it was understood that there would be no official support in the case of any legal claim. Life was sometimes made difficult for such privateers who found themselves under unwarranted scrutiny by their own authorities when Elizabeth's government went through one of its periodic bouts of back-stabbing. On the other hand, privateers walked a narrow line and were often their worst enemy when they stepped over it.

The successive captains of the Isle of Wight seem to have been up to their necks in organized piracy. Edward Horsey, whose family lie buried in Carisbrooke church presided over the Island at a time (1565-83) when Spain in particular was becoming highly suspicious of privateers operating in the area. Horsey had the unique distinction of being Captain of the Wight and Vice-Admiral, so all matters pertaining to local piracy came his way and he was able to take delaying tactics to unprecedented lengths. In the summer of 1581, Elizabeth's spymaster, Francis Walsingham, reported from the Admiralty Court, quoting the unlikely-named Julius Caesar, an Admiralty Judge, that 'it appeareth that the Isle of Wyght is a great favourer of pyrates which groweth principally through the corruption of Sir Ed. Horsey's Lieutenant ...'

This seems to have been a bit of buck-passing, as a 'projector' (agent) called John Johnson had already reported to Lord Burghley, the Queen's chief minister, that large numbers of well-connected gentlemen regularly consorted with pirates, even if Horsey himself was clever enough not to get too directly involved.

His successor, George Carey (Captain 1585-1603) was in an even more useful position. As well as holding the same two posts as Horsey, he was related both to the Lord High Admiral, Howard of Effingham and hero of the Armada and to the Queen herself. Given the state of open warfare during his Captaincy, Carey had no qualms about taking a Spanish ship, renaming her *Commander* and flying his own colours from her mast. One of the Newport town drums was used to beat the crew to quarters. The Island gentry did not take this lying down. They presented Carey with a 'remonstrance', a 'little Bill of Rights' as Richard Worsley described it in 1781 ... 'and we demand that pyracie, robberie and such like, tending to the utter discredit of the country and the displeasure of Almighty God, may be abolished.'

George Carey, Governor of the Isle of Wight, was also a friend of pirates. The author

Below these two, captains and gentlemen of the Wight operated under their safety. Edward Denny did not own land on the Island but he used the place as a safe haven for his piracy. In September 1577 he brought a French and a Spanish ship into one of the harbours, only to have them impounded by Horsey, for once playing it by the book and was forced to appear before Burghley's Privy Council to explain himself. He had to sell one of the ships to buy his way out of trouble.

John Vaughan, referred to as 'the pirate Vaughan' in various dispatches from the Spanish ambassador to Philip II, was master of the 60 ton *Bowe* and lived in such an impressive house in Newport that it counted for local tax purposes as two. No stranger to the courts because of his short fuse, Vaughan appeared before the town's bailiffs, William Porter and John Serle in November 1568 charged with wounding sailor Edward Clayse with his dagger. Duels like this had been illegal under Elizabeth. Ten years later, encompassing in one incident the extraordinary duality of the privateers, Vaughan professed ignorance of the delivery of a cargo of salt at his Newport house on the excuse that he was away at the time on a diplomatic mission to the Netherlands. By 1581 Vaughan had four ships, each one armed to the teeth and capable of taking all but the largest galleons of Spain.

Next in the pirate pecking order came the merchant-captains who acted as distributors of stolen goods. Thomas Page had become captain of Carey's *Commander* by 1590 and had his own receiving warehouse along Newport Quay. Like the far more notorious thief-taker Jonathan Wild in a later generation London, Page ran with the hare and the hounds by becoming town bailiff in 1595. Local butcher John Hallett pulled no punches however when he described Page as a 'raskall, rogue, knave, thief' to the man's face. Henry Joliffe was another Newport merchant who did not ask where his goods came from – or in some cases, knew perfectly well. In 1575 he was master of the 200 ton *Castle of Comfort*, operating under the licence of the Prince of Condé and shared warehouses with another merchant-fence, Richard Markes. At the end of the 1580s and almost certainly with the backing of Sir Edward Horsey, Joliffe was attacking French and Spanish ships in the Channel and the Irish Sea.

Below these men of status and substance was a sub-culture about which we know very little. We have a smattering of names, some of which can still be found in the Island. Bailey and White appeared before bailiffs in 1574; Austen and Daye in 1577. Yards, Gaskins, Whites, Fosters, Corporalls, Sawyers, Bords, Pierces, Nutshavens and Hoopers litter the piratical annals of the time. And they had their own lair – at Mead Hole.

In July 1570, Edward Horsey, perhaps a little concerned that his masters in London might be on to him, carried out an inventory of ships moored in this anchorage between East Cowes and Wootton Creek. Today, the area is very secluded as it is the private beach attached to Osborne House where Queen Victoria braved the waters from her bathing machine. It lay a mile west of Shofleet Creek with 'fair landing at full sea three quarters of a mile towards the east at a fathom water and at low water dry and oozy.' Horsey was rather alarmed to find ten French men-of-war anchored there 'well trimmed in warlike order and aboard them as I can learn 300 of their nation as well mariners as others.'

Like the more notorious pirate refuge of Maracaibo in the West Indies a century later, Mead Hole was a hell on earth and its name had become generic. A fishmonger from Southampton swore that his eels were come by honestly in 1577, that they were 'no Mead Hole goods nor thief-stolen.'

The Spanish ambassador sent an intelligencer (spy) to the area in the same year as Horsey's sail-count. His report is an astonishing list of contraband goods and a hive of activity. Much of it was plundered from Spanish ships, including wine, soap, oil, wood, saffron and other spices. Eleven years later, it had grown and a witness saw over thirty vessels moored there. The sailors wore flashy hose and doublets, wearing gold chains and whistles around their necks. Shoemakers operated there, so did goldsmiths, brewers, bakers and butchers. It is likely that some of those dealers came from the mainland, but many of them would have been Cowes and Newport men, doing a brisk trade in stolen goods.

It is uncertain when this heyday of piracy came to an end. George Carey was certainly the last Captain to condone it and his passing, along with his queen in 1603, saw the end of an era. The last recorded arrival of a prize ship taken by a privateer was brought into Cowes by Captain Scras in 1629. Its cargo spoke of the future. The days of wool, hides, oil and soap had gone. Scras' booty was from a new world indeed – sugar and tobacco.

Chapter 4

The Sinking of the *Mary Rose*

T he religious service that was held in the church of St Helens on Sunday 19 July 1545 must have been a bizarre one. Even without the upheavals of recent years, which had seen first the king, Henry VIII, then his entire people, excommunicated from Rome and the destruction of the Island's religious houses including the abbey at Quarr, men's minds cannot have been wholly on God on that Sunday.

Today, all that remains of the church is a white painted tower – the nave and chancel have gone – and it stands on the sea at the entrance to Bembridge harbour. In the 1540s of course, it was complete, surrounded by a churchyard and fishing village. What made the service bizarre, no matter what kind of Catholic-Protestant hybrid variant was going on inside, was the view from the churchyard.

It must have been possible to see, weighing anchor in St Helens roads, two hundred and twenty five warships of the fleet of the French king, François 1, on their way to capture Portsmouth and begin an invasion of England.

The more enlightened Islanders, the Governor and the gentry, would have seen this moment coming for years. Henry VII had attempted to smash any potential Franco-Spanish alliance by marrying two of his sons,

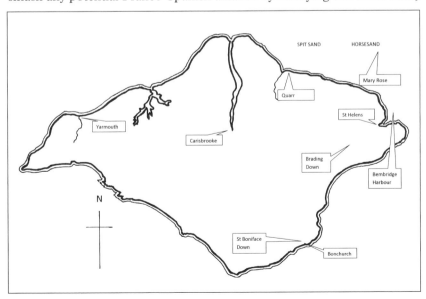

Location map 4. The author

The entrance to Bembridge harbour today from the St Helens side. The French fleet of François I, including galleasses and galleys, rounded the headland in the centre of the picture on its way to attack Portsmouth Harbour. Carol Trow

one after the other, to the same Spanish princess, Catherine of Aragon, but the scheme had failed and for the first year of his reign, his successor, Henry VIII, had been building up a fleet and strengthening the fortifications along the south coast.

Many local labourers must have been involved in the creation of fortresses on either side of the Medina at East and West Cowes, others to the west in Yarmouth and the east along Sandown Bay. Curiously, there was no noticeable alteration to Carisbrooke Castle, whose fourteenth-century 'state of the art' defences were now three hundred years out of date. Henry ordered that each parish on the Island should pay for the purchase of a cannon. Five of these have survived; one, in Carisbrooke Castle's museum, is dated 1549 and was a falcon made by the Owen brothers of London. Its maximum range was about ¾ mile, but it was only truly effective at 300 yards.

In the shifting sands of European diplomacy, Henry had launched an invasion of France to capture Boulogne successfully in the summer of 1544, during a temporary spat between France and Spain. By the following Spring however, the European superpowers had kissed and made up and François launched a two-pronged attack, the first – and more important – was to drive the English out of Boulogne and the second, perhaps always something of a feint, to destroy Henry's ships at anchor in Portsmouth harbour.

Those anxiously watching from both sides of the Solent on that hot, bright, windless July day could not have known that the French fleet, huge though it was, had suffered its own disaster. A fire had broken out on board the French flagship, the 800 ton *Carraquon*, soon after a party in which François bade farewell to his commanders. The fleet commander, Claude d'Annebault, transferred to *La Maitresse*, only to have that ship run aground off the French coast at Honfleur. All in all, it was not a good beginning.

Henry, as commander-in-chief of all his forces, sea and land, had camped with a force of 12000 men on what is today Southsea Common. He was expecting reinforcements from the West County and the Thames and had they arrived on time, could have caught the French in a neat pincer movement in the Solent. As it was, all he had in Portsmouth harbour was a motley assembly of warships – carracks, galleys and galleasses, commanded by John Dudley, Viscount Lisle; perhaps sixty ships.

The king dined with his captains on board the flagship, the Henry *Grace à Dieu* and presented Sir George Carew with the official whistle and chain which were the insignia of a vice-admiral. He was to command the king's second ship, the *Mary Rose*.

The first we hear of this ship is in 1511 when she was built, along with the *Peter Pomegranate* and nearly twenty others, but in 1536, she underwent an extensive refit which increased her firing capacity and made her a modern warship in every respect. The date is significant. This was the year in which Quarr Abbey was demolished and its lands sold off; it is highly likely that the *Mary Rose* was refitted with Island money.

A detailed inventory of what the ship carried comes from the Anthony Roll, ironically not completed until the year after she sank (or perhaps as part of her salvage operations). The list of ordinance, brass and iron guns, included cannons, demi-cannons, culverins, sakers and falcons, portpieces, slings and demi-slings and hailshots. Stone, lead and iron shot was on board, as well as the old English standby for boarding purposes and close-quarter work, 250 yew longbows, six grass bowstrings, pikes, bills and darts. The *Mary Rose* weighed 700 tons and was supposed to carry a crew of 185 soldiers, 200 sailors and 30 gunners, a total of 415. It is likely that, on 19 July, the total number exceeded 700 and in that lay a clue to what might have happened.

The previous day, when the French fleet had first arrived in the Solent, a number of English ships had gone out to meet them. The deep water

The only known depiction of the Mary Rose *from the Anthony Roll, 1546.* The author

channel into the harbour is tricky and explains what many tourists find a rather circuitous route to the Island today. Negotiating the hidden sand banks of the Horse Spit and No Man's Land, both sides opened fire. Martin du Bellay, serving with the French cavalry, wrote, 'After a long fight with gunshot the enemy began to ship to the left to the shelter of the land.' Nearly a century later, Islander Sir John Oglander, then deputy Governor of Portsmouth, refers to the same event – 'it is true we were too weak and withdrew to the Horse.'

The clash of arms had exposed the lack of firepower of the English and at dawn on the Sunday, D'Annebault took advantage of the relative lack of wind and sailed for the harbour entrance, sending ahead his fast galleys, which were not only independent of the wind, but sufficiently low in the water to provide difficult targets for the English gunners. The idea was to give the English a slap in the face and lure them out to fight in the Solent, away from the back-up of the shore batteries along the Southsea Front.

'Fortune favoured our fleet,' D'Annebault recorded later, 'in this manner [the galleys' attack] for about an hour during which time, among other damages the English received, the *Mary Rose*, one of their principal ships, was sunk by our cannon and of five or six hundred men which were on board only five and thirty escaped.'

This is either French propaganda or a genuine belief that French gunfire had sunk the ship. Either way it was not true. Peter Carew, whose family were directly involved, was an eyewitness and at a much closer distance that D'Annebault. The French galleys made straight for the *Grace à Dieu*, from which the king's flag fluttered. Seeing this, George Carew on board the *Mary Rose* sailed to the flagship's aid. The ship began to keel or list to port as it turned to engage the galleys. Carew, alarmed at the angle of tilt, called his ship's master to him and asked him what was going on. The answer is not recorded. Gawaine Carew, George's uncle, sailing alongside on the 600 ton *Matthew Gronson* called out to the vice admiral what the problem was. George Carew's enigmatic answer has remained unexplained until now. He shouted back to Gawaine that 'he had the sort of knaves whom he could not rule'. Gawaine's interpretation of this is odd – 'He had in the ship a hundred mariners, the worst of them being able to be master in the best ship within the realm and those so maligned and distained one another that refusing to do that which they should do, were careless to do that which they ought to do and so

Vice Admiral George Carew was in command of the Mary Rose *and went down with the ship in the summer of 1545.* The author

Now the home of the Royal Yacht Squadron, this was the site of Henry VIII's fort at West Cowes - the low wall to the right of the ivy-clad building is part of the original breastworks. Carol Trow

contending in envy perished in frowardness.'

Perish they did. The Mary Rose sank with astonishing speed, water crashing in through her open gun ports and flooding the lower decks. The guns rolled free of their housings, splintering the carvel-built timbers of the hull and unfired shot shifted the ballast so quickly that only a handful of the crew were able to escape.

While a disbelieving crowd watched from the shore at Southsea and the king rode backwards and forwards, furious at his inability to do anything, only the mast heads stood above water and the French no doubt, cheered wildly.

'Oh my pretty men,' Henry is said to have groaned, 'oh, my gentlemen. Drowned like rattens.'

The rest of the battle was inconclusive, with no further disaster or indeed triumph. As if to underline the fact that the French invasion was actually nothing of the sort, the enemy fleet turned tail, but not before they vented their fury on the Isle of Wight.

The preparations made by the Militia, apart from the culverins in each parish, included the building of beacons on high ground around the

The old church, St Helens. Erosion has destroyed the nave and churchyard, but the congregation would have seen the French fleet in the Solent from here in 1545. Carol Trow

Island. The total population cannot have exceeded nine thousand, but every man was, to an extent, his own militiaman, expected to practise with bow and billhook on a regular basis. Every male adult was obliged to serve and there is some evidence to suggest that at least some of the archers were women.

In command of the reinforcement troops from Hampshire and Wiltshire, Sir Edward Bellingham worked hand in glove with the Captain of the Island, Sir Richard Worsley. Between them they had perhaps six thousand fighting men, but they had to be scattered all over the Island, especially if the vast French fleet broke up and decided to land anywhere around the coast. Eight hundred and fifty Wiltshire men had been dispatched to the west, to guard the fort at Yarmouth and watch the narrow Lymington crossing. A further two hundred and fifty were dragooned into a frantic speeding up of the building of the castle at Sandown, still, that summer, unfinished. The bulk of Worsley's force was strung out from Brading Down to St Boniface Down and their obsolete, sometimes home-made weapons were a reminder, if one were needed, that the Islanders possessed no standing army in times of national emergency like this.

The French attacked in three waves, rowing boats being towed close to land by the numerable galleys. The first, commanded by an Italian *condottiere* (mercenary), Pieto Strozzi attacked St Helens fort, whose guns had been raking the French fleet with cannon fire for several hours. The defenders were driven out, scattering into the hinterland of Bembridge harbour. The oncoming French burned the tiny fishing hamlets of Seaview and Nettlestone and destroyed the manor of Woolverton as well as the more sizeable village of St Helens.

Further south in Bonchurch, Seigneur de Tais, Colonel-General of the Infantry, brought his troops ashore to find no opposition. This was a tactical mistake on Worsley's part as men laden with armour and equipment floundering at the water's edge were an easier mark than on dry land. The Militia had taken up position flanked by thick reeds and cliffs. Today it is difficult to know exactly where this would have been and again the English, probably outnumbered and certainly outfought, fell back. A local commander, Captain Fischer, offered one hundred pounds for anyone who could find him a horse. Surrounded by the French, he was never heard of again.

Strategically, the bay at Sandown offered the French the easiest landing point and because the fort was incomplete, there was little to stop them. Led by galley captains, Pierrebon and Marsay, the invaders landed and began to deploy. Worsley and Bellingham however were alive to the great danger. Two hours march would bring the French to Newport and the heart of the Island. The biggest clash came on the low sand dunes, more or less where the Island's zoo now stands and with both their leaders wounded, the French fell back to their ships.

Then the Militia turned north to deal with Strozzi's troops who had got themselves marooned on the Bembridge Spit. Grabbing every available horse and donkey, Worsley organised a ramshackle cavalry force and charged uphill, driving the astonished French off Culver Head and back to smouldering Bembridge.

Here the French infantry made a defiant stand and du Tais arrived from the south to organize a dignified withdrawal. The greatest loss to d'Annebault was the death of a galley captain, Pierre de Blacas, who was brought down by an arrow in the knee as his men took on board fresh water for the journey home. Attempting to offer himself for ransom, which was the European custom for gentlemen on the battlefield, a Militiaman smashed in his skull; clearly he was unaware of the rules of engagement.

So what happened to the *Mary Rose* that balmy July day so long ago? Walter Ralegh, one of the most famous and experienced of the Devon 'sea dogs' of the next generation believed the ship had a design fault so that fast handling of the type she attempted in the Solent was bound to end in disaster. Ralegh had obviously not read the reports of Admiral Sir Edward Howard in 1513. He had commanded the *Mary Rose* in battle and in what today we would call speed trials. He wrote to Henry VIII in September of that year, 'The Mary Rose, Sir, she is the noblest ship of sail and as great a ship at this hour that I trow [believe] to be in Christendom. A ship of one hundred tons will not be sooner about than she.'

In other words, the *Mary Rose* could turn on a sixpence and outrun any other ship he had.

An enquiry was set up immediately at the end of July 1545. The Admiral, Lisle and Charles Bowden, Duke of Suffolk, who had been with Henry when the *Mary Rose* went down, spoke to Peter Carew and decided that 'indiscipline and handling' were responsible. All of this puts the onus squarely on George Carew and his unruly knaves.

If we analyse Gawaine Carew's explanation, it makes little sense. He comments that the *Mary Rose*'s crew were such expert sailors that they were all trying to impress each other and would not co-operate. In reality – and especially in shot of the enemy – the reverse would be true; they would actually try to out do each other in skill and competence. We know that the Tudor navy was not composed of angels. Many of the sailors were pressed men from seaports all over the country. They were murderers, thieves and drunkards, but the threat of the lash as punishment and the camaradie that comes with serving on the same ship and being responsible for others' lives goes a long way to overcoming that.

The most recent research however may well be a better – and the correct – explanation. Extensive scientific analysis of the skeletons found in the ship's hull when it was raised from the sea-bed in October 1982 has established that nearly two thirds of them were southern European, probably Spanish. This is not too surprising. Foreign experts were constantly being called in to provide technical know how, especially in military matters. Belgians, Hans Poppenruyter and Simon Giles were making cannons for Henry in 1514; so was Frenchman Peter Bande in the 1520s. When the notoriously tight-pursed Elizabeth at last consented to spend some money to upgrade Carisbrooke Castle in the 1590s, it was the Italian military architect, Federigo Gianibelli who got the contract.

Mercenaries were common place everywhere in Europe. Professor Hugh Montgomery of University College, London speculates that the European crewmen were either pressed ex-prisoners of war or men who fought for the highest bidder. 'In the chaos of battle, with all the shooting and guns going off, it would have taken a very clear chain of command and a very disciplined well-rehearsed crew to close the gun port lids in time.'

The DNA skeletal evidence is incontrovertible, but it still raises issues. Why would an experienced naval man like George Carew trust a capital ship like the *Mary Rose* to non-English speaking sailors when the enemy were at the gate? That too, makes little sense.

One thing however is certain. As the French sailed away through St Helen's Roads that summer of 1545, the Isle of Wight would never see invasion again.

Chapter 5

Insula Infortunata

One of the Island's lights in Stuart England was Sir John Oglander, whose family had held lands at Nunwell since the thirteenth century. At the age of twenty, he was made a Justice of the Peace 'when I not well understood myself or place and was ashamed to sit on the Bench as not having hair on my face and less wit'.

If a man carried out his duties efficiently, the role of Justice was a huge job. He was the workhorse of the executive, responsible for the collection of taxes, control of the militia as well as sitting as a magistrate presiding over court cases. Such men were always landowners, so had estates to manage as well.

By the late 1630s, by which time Charles I had dispensed with the services of his annoying parliament and was in the throes of the 'eleven years' tyranny', Oglander was a knight, had been Governor of Portsmouth, MP for Yarmouth and was High Sheriff of Hampshire. He had a large family and lived through the tension and strife which characterised the Civil War on the Island (See Chapter 6).

Oglander is important in Island criminal affairs because he kept a diary or commonplace book. This chapter examines his view of the Island in the early seventeenth century as 'Insula Infortunata' – the unfortunate Island.

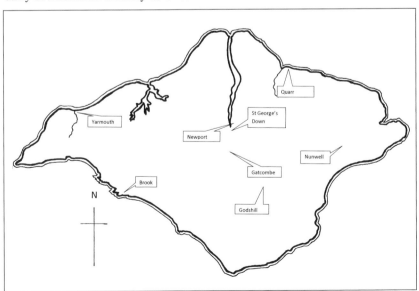

Location Map 5. The author

In common with everywhere else, the Isle of Wight suffered periodic outbreaks of serious epidemics. In 1627 smallpox was brought by 'young Urry of Gatcombe', culminating in over 2000 cases and several hundred deaths. It would be another 170 years before a cure was found.

Among much wise advice given to his children, Oglander warned them to be wary of lawyers, quite possibly, his own distant cousin, also John, who lived in Newport. 'Be advised by me,' the Lord of Nunwell wrote, 'have no suits in law.' Members of the legal profession were regarded, like moneylenders, as a necessary evil. Unlike true scholars, they had no university (their training grounds were the London Inns of Court) and they were seen as parasites. Oglander records that in the days of George Carey's Captaincy of the Island (1585-1603) a lawyer was forced off the Island 'with a pound of lighted candles hanging at his breeches and bells about his legs.' Traditionally, bell, book and candle were used by the Godly to ward off evil spirits.

The late 1620s seemed a grim time to Oglander. Not only was smallpox taking its toll, but economic recession hit which contrasted with earlier years and the older generation looked back to the days of 'good Queen Bess', Oglander among them.

The machinations of James I and his son Charles, together with the political hot-headedness of the Duke of Buckingham (stabbed to death in Portsmouth in 1628) led to war with both France and Spain and a Scottish regiment, commanded by the Earl of Merton, was stationed in the Island. We have a fascinating glimpse of the Highlanders seen through the eyes of a refined gentleman from the far south. Their sole diet was oaten cakes, milk, cheese, butter and porridge and they seemed not to know how to cut meat or bread. Fifteen hundred of them were billeted in and around Newport on the way to the Ile de Rhé, but they did not actually leave until 3 September 1628.

Oglander, along with most of the Island, was furious. 'They not only committed diverse murders, but also became a terror to the inhabitants.' As a JP, Oglander knew his law. Billeting was illegal – and one of the many charges to be laid against Charles I in the years ahead. Next time, Oglander promised, the free men of the Isle of Wight would die fighting the 'Scotch regiment' on the shore.

'By the inconveniences that followed,' he wrote, 'murders, rapes, robberies, burglaries, the getting of bastards and almost the undoing of the whole Island' left at best a nasty taste in the mouth. It was also left an estimated seventy illegitimate children to add to the Island's economic woes.

Oglander gives us one or two glimpses of Island criminal life. He fulminates against drunkenness rather as his former king had against tobacco. Perhaps he spoke from the experience of his court when he wrote 'of all vices, hate drunkenness. [It] damneth both body and soul into hell-fire'.

On 3 July 1632, the militia were drilling on St George's Down near Newport when a volley of musket fire accidentally killed Sampson Saphier, a local shopkeeper. Acting as coroner, Oglander examined him. 'No skin was broken, but certainly all the nerves and sinews in the poll of his head were either broken off or, with the fire, shrunk up and his brain turned in his head.' He is probably describing *contre-coup*, a situation in which Saphier fell with the shock of musket balls narrowly missing him and hitting his head as he went down, causing fatal brain damage.

Three months earlier, Oglander's own deputy, the Lieutenant-Governor Sir Edward Dennys had a row with Philip Fleming, later Steward of the Island 'in the open street ... beat one another with their sticks and from thence came to cuffs, to their own shame.'

Oglander does not record the outcome, but two months before this had been sued by a couple who appeared before him for keeping 'an ale house without licence and suspected a bawdy house'. If the accusation was correct, then George King and his wife were running a brothel in Shorwell (perhaps today's Crown Inn) which ran contrary to the magistrate's puritan sensibilities. The Kings tried it on and the case went all the way to the notorious Star Chamber in London, where cases were heard in camera and there was no jury. Oglander was acquitted of wrong doing and both King and his wife were sentenced to be whipped.

Since the Commonplace Book was a private diary, never intended for publication, Oglander was candid about his neighbours. The Bowerman family of Brook had been leading lights in Island affairs for generations. Thomas Bowerman's great-grandfather, says Oglander, was 'most barbarously murdered' by two of his tenants. The men lay in wait for him by the large pond on his estate, robbed him and threw him into a ditch. But they hadn't done the job properly and Bowerman was able to crawl back home. He lingered for nine days and in that time recognized his assailants who came to see how he was. If they intended somehow to finish the job, they had no opportunity, because they were charged, found guilty and subsequently confessed. The more prominent member of the two who had wanted to feed Bowerman to his pigs, was hanged 'on Gallobury' the site of one of the Island's gibbets, near Calbourne.

Another Island family, the Gardes of Godshill, originally from France, stole cattle and disguised them by softening their horns with hot bread to twist them out of shape. To a man, the family were 'sly, dishonest and given to filching'.

Unhappy with his lot as he sometimes was, Oglander's over-arching advice to his children was this – 'If ever thou desirest to live plentifully, out of debt, worshipfully and with the respect of thy neighbours and the inhabitants, settle thyself to live in the Island and roam not out of it.'

Perhaps that point of view would change with the 'world turned upside down' in the summer of 1642.

Chapter 6

'That Man of Blood'

The power struggle between king and parliament that had been simmering ever since Charles I became king erupted into open warfare, debatably, on Monday, 22 August 1642 when he raised his standard at Nottingham.

The country as a whole polarised into regional factions – royalist or parliamentarian – with both sides anxious to grab what money, ships, weapons and other military equipment they could. Control of the ports was vital, so all eyes were on Portsmouth, long a major naval base and early in August, a sizeable Parliamentarian fleet was concentrating in the Solent.

In those early weeks, the Island's gentry followed a path pursued by many others around the country. Twenty-two of them signed a declaration to the effect that they saw it as their duty to protect 'the peace of this Island' against foreign incursion, papists and 'other ill affected persons'. Parliament decided to read this as a mild form of sedition and three of the Island's six MPs were called to London to be sent for as 'Delinquents' to explain their actions.

'Thou wouldst think it strange,' John Oglander wrote later, 'if I should tell thee there was a time in England when brothers killed brothers,

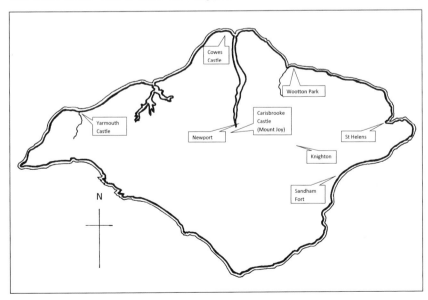

Location Map 6. The author

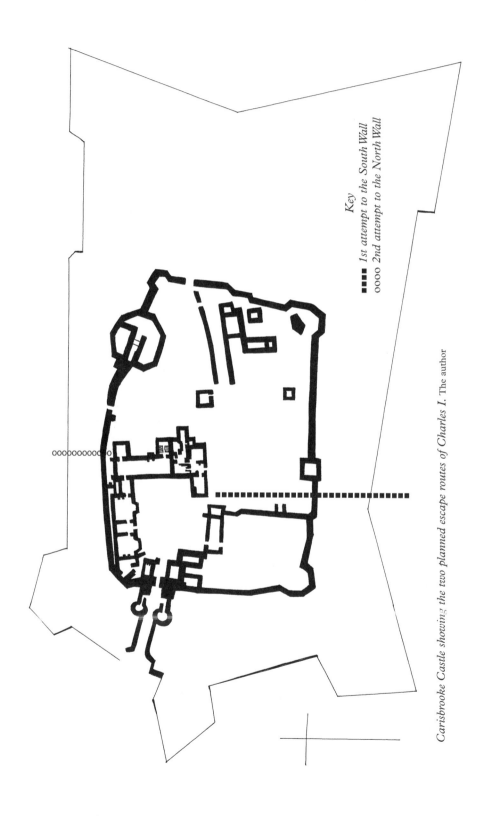

Carisbrooke Castle showing the two planned escape routes of Charles I. The author

cousins, cousins and friends their friends. Nay, when they conceived it was no offence to commit murder. To murder a man held less offence than to kill a dog ... When thou wentest to bed at night, thou knowest not whether thou shouldst be murdered afore day.'

As events moved on, the Island's polarisation was as follows: Newport, with its militant mayor, Moses Read, was for the Parliament; Carisbrooke castle and the other four forts were for the king; the ordinary Islanders probably remained ambivalent, although there were a few hot-heads on both sides.

At Cowes castle, Captain Humphrey Turney was so furious at the presence of Parliamentarian warships in the Solent that he fired two cannon from the rampart walls himself, sending his shot snarling over the bows of the *Lion*, commanded by Captain Ramsey. In the days that followed, Turney would find his fort ringed by Parliamentarian musketeers and under house arrest while his command was taken from him.

At Yarmouth castle, Captain John Burley refused to surrender without written authorisation from the king. This was clearly not forthcoming as Charles was miles away in Nottingham and had his hands full. Burley surrendered without firing a shot on 22 August.

Captain Brutus Bucke, in command at the newly rebuilt Sandham fort was actually off the Island on 18 August when his mutinous crew surrendered. When Bucke came back, he was placed under arrest in his own fortress.

Most of the interest lay geographically at the heart of the Island however. Newport was staunchly Parliamentarian, but the biggest arsenal, of cannon, gunpowder and the most of the militia's sidearms were under the control of Royalist Carisbrooke Castle. Henry VIII's cannon were still in situ in various Island parishes and in case these should be hauled out of cold storage (it had, after all, been half a century since they were last needed) some of them were sabotaged by Royalists.

In command at Carisbrooke was Colonel Jeremy Brett described by his opponents as 'swaggering' and of 'rude speech' who had been put in command of the whole Island by the king. On Monday 15 August, Brett decided to stamp his authority on the Island by arresting Moses Read in Newport. At his back were the leading Royalists, Turney and Bucke, the fort commanders, Sir John Oglander of Nunwell and Robert Dillington of Knighton. Read was not at home, but the Newport mob threatened and jostled the party, calling them 'villains', 'traitors' and 'Papists'. For their own safety, the Royalists went to an inn – perhaps the Castle in the High Street – to plan what to do next. Brett wrote later to Read, 'I shall hardly come thither [to Newport] again until you have put the town into a more civil posture ... I cannot compare your town to anything but to a large Bedlam.'

By 24 August, Brett's beleaguered garrison in the castle at Carisbrooke had little choice but to surrender. With naval troops ashore and reinforcements from the mainland under the command of Captain Swanley, about 600 men were camped on the neighbouring hill of Mount Joy (now a cemetery), where they proceeded to roast the sheep they had already prevented from being driven into the castle to feed the garrison. Brett had perhaps twenty fighting men and far more women and children and duly surrendered under safe conduct.

For the next four years, there was a great deal of tension in the Island but little actual involvement in the war that raged on the mainland. Sixteen sailors were charged with sacking the house of royalist Sir William Hopkins in St Helens. These men threatened to do the same to other country houses too and they were imprisoned at Cowes Castle; not perhaps the best move as the place had no locks or bolts at the time!

Rumours of greater trouble led to the imprisonment (twice) in London of John Oglander, just for being a known royalist. He arrived in London on 29 January 1643 and stayed in Cabbage Lane, Westminster for three weeks. Here he was under house arrest and for a further four weeks at the *Seven Stars* in the Strand before he could buy his release. It was while he was there that Oglander's wife, Frances, died of smallpox and the entry in his diary is written in his blood. When his son George died later, he wrote the first entry with his tears. The size of the Newport town watch was also increased; their nightly passwords have survived in the town's records.

By 1646 Charles, outfought by Parliament's New Model Army, outmanoeuvred and broke, was forced to surrender. Much of his time was now spent at Hampton Court while Parliament tried to work out some kind of *modus vivendi* with him after the bewildering events of the last four years.

On Saturday 14 November 1647, the Island's new governor, twenty-six-year-old Colonel Robert Hammond was riding down the steep hill from the castle to Newport when he was stopped by two gentlemen. They introduced themselves as John Ashburton and John Berkely and asked Hammond if he knew who was nearby. The governor did not know how to answer this cryptic question, so Berkely told him – 'Even good King Charles, who is come from Hampton Court for fear of being murdered privately.'

Hammond nearly fell off his horse! He was now placed in a very difficult position. On the one hand he was a cousin of Oliver Cromwell, by this time the most powerful man in the country, as second-in-command of the New Model Army with and a huge following in the Commons. On the other

Martyr or traitor? Charles I was under house arrest at Carisbrooke Castle and tried to escape twice. His daughter, Elizabeth died there. From the portrait by Van Dyke. The author

hand, Hammond's uncle Henry was the king's chaplain. Charles' reasons for wanting refuge in the Island are unclear. Expecting support from the Island in 1642, he had not got it. Perhaps he saw the place as some kind of springboard from which he could relaunch the war, a magnet for the thousands of disgruntled cavaliers who wandered the countryside.

There is even a theory that Cromwell himself engineered Charles' flight to the Island so that he could escape quietly to the continent and a difficult dilemma be solved.

Charles was brought from Titchfield, the Earl of Southampton's home in Hampshire and spent his first night in the Island at Cowes' only decent in The Plume of Feathers. In gilt letters on his headboard was the Biblical text *Remember Thy End*. As he rode through Newport, the nascent royalists lined the route and cheered him; Frances Trattle rushed forward and presented him with a rose. John Oglander, old and ill from his imprisonment, 'could do nothing but sigh and weep for two nights and a day'. To him, Charles Stuart – 'that man of blood' as his enemies called him – was riding, smiling, into a death trap. The Island, wrote Oglander, 'was the Paradise of England, and now, Anno 1647, it is just like the other parts of the Kingdom, a melancholy, dijected, sad place ...' Above all, Oglander lamented the passing, for ever, of the great days of the landowners. 'Ringwood, of Newport, the pedlar; Maynard, the apothecary; Matthews the baker; Wavell and Legge, farmers ... these ruled the whole Island.'

At first, the king's time on the Island saw him being given a great deal of freedom. His furniture was brought from Hampton Court. He hunted in Parkhurst forest, played bowls on the open drill area to the east of the castle (still called the Bowling Green to this day) and had regular visitors and correspondence from half the country, it seemed. Even so, Charles was accompanied everywhere and a guard was posted outside his bedroom door above the Great Chamber. The castle gates were locked.

The king wrote to parliament demanding a treaty be drawn up in his presence in London. The answer – eventually – was a commission led by the Earl of Denbigh who arrived at the castle on Christmas Eve 1647 and discussed issues with the king in the Great Chamber. On Christmas Day – at that time an ordinary working day like any other – other visitors arrived; this time, from Scotland. With them, Charles hatched a Scots invasion and a series of English uprisings which would, in effect, become the second civil war. There were strings attached, of course. Charles had to recognize the Solemn League and Covenant which had abolished bishops; he had to accept the Presbyterian faith in England and to work more closely with Scotland. Two copies were made of this document – one hidden in the king's chamber at the castle; the other buried, at least temporarily, in a lead-lined container in somebody's garden. This was because visitors to the castle were routinely searched. Charles now effectively told the parliamentary commissioners what they could do with their proposals, which left him with no power at all.

While Colonel Hammond saw the furious Denbigh off the premises, the king actively planned his first escape attempt. He was actually putting on his riding boots to go hunting – during which he would, in fact, gallop to the coast – when Hammond returned. The sensible, rational, humane gaoler was no more. He probably felt betrayed by the king, feared for his own position and perhaps even his life at the hands of Denbigh's commissioners and ordered an immediate crackdown. All Charles' personal retinue was to leave the Island – and that included Hammond's own uncle, the royal chaplain.

While they were riding out through Newport, Captain John Burley, the royalist who had been forced to surrender his fort five years earlier, grabbed the town drum and banged it so furiously that a large crowd assembled. Burley promised to lead the mob against the castle to free the king by force, chanting 'For God, the king and the people!' In the event, it was largely hot air. Burley was arrested and sent to Winchester on charges of treason. He was found guilty and executed. The contemporary account of his trial is among the Stuart papers at Carisbrooke Castle.

Parliament, now increasingly dominated by the New Model Army, acted with speed and efficiency. Seven extra warships were sent to the Solent and fifty barrels of gunpowder sent to Carisbrooke. Such was the personal charisma of Charles, however, that he won over waverers in the new household Hammond had set up and escape plans were re-hatched in earnest.

All sorts of ideas were discussed. A daylight assault of the Burley type was unlikely to succeed because of Gianibelli's defences and the stock of weaponry at the garrison's disposal. Other suggestions might have worked – Charles disguised as a coalman or washerwoman sneaking past the sentries on the gate. Another variant had him escaping while a fire was started in the building and the king would simply vanish in the smoke and confusion.

Clearly all this subterfuge could only work with help from the outside and regular correspondence between the king and his would-be rescuers. This was where Mary came in. We do not have her surname, but she was a laundress, presumably from Carisbrooke village or Newport and she had access to the king's quarters. She hid letters under his carpet and would collect his replies from the same place the next day. No doubt she convinced the guard that she detested the prisoner and gave them no cause to doubt her. Henry Firebrace was another agent. As Charles' groom of the bedchamber, he had plenty of opportunity, not only to talk to the king in private, but to study the castle's layout.

On March 20 1648 everything was in place. Waiting until dark, Charles was to squeeze past the bars of his window in the southern end of the Great Chamber building and shin down a rope smuggled in by Firebrace. The guard outside the king's locked bedroom would have no idea what was going on and there were no sentries in the courtyard below. Once on the ground, the king would use the cover of darkness to cross to one of the towers on the south curtain wall, timing his run to elude the patrolling guards and abseil down the wall to the waiting horse supplied by Edward Worsley and Richard Osborne. From there the three would gallop through the night and the open country to a waiting ship off the coast at Wootton Park (between East Cowes and Ryde) waiting for a favourable

The Grammar School at Newport, the scene in 1648 of the meeting between the Parliamentary commissioners and King Charles I. Today, it is a youth club. Carol Trow

wind to France. There, John Newbold waited with a 'lusty boat ... at the seaside.'

The only problem – and it has passed into legend – was the size of the window. The king had declined Firebrace's offer of a file for the bars on the grounds that it would make too much noise and that presumably, he thought he was slim enough to squeeze through anyway. Waiting on the stones below the Great Chamber, lurking in the shadows, Firebrace heard the window open and the rattle as the rope was uncoiled down the wall. Then, nothing. Eventually, after several minutes, a candle appeared at the window – the signal that something was wrong. Firebrace dashed to the south wall and scared off the waiting royalists by a shower of pebbles. Worsley and Osborne mounted and rode into the darkness without their king.

Embarrassingly for Hammond, the information about this failed escape was written down by the king and intercepted by parliament's spy network, the Derby House Committee. Cromwell himself sent a version of it to his cousin, who attempted to save face by dismissing everybody, including Firebrace. The king was moved to new quarters, this time overlooking the North wall, whose ramparts and the hill below were far steeper than the relatively easy south. Below the new bedroom window, Hammond built a wooden sentry platform which was manned twenty four hours a day.

Since bars had defeated the king before, this time he was ready. There were already clever gadgets on the market for this purpose, like Captain Ramelli's 'Great Force' or 'Endless Screw', a steel winding contraption that forced bars apart. Unable to obtain one of these, Charles had to settle for acid. Via Firebrace, who had at this stage not yet left, he contacted a locksmith called Farmer in Bow Lane, London, who supplied *aqua fortis*, a solution of nitric acid, which would burn through iron.

This time it worked a treat. But this time, human fallibility played a part. The guards on the platform below had been bribed to look the other way while the king hopped down past them and shinned down the rope to the same loyal supporters waiting with horses below. The only problem was that those guards had been changed by Hammond at the last moment and Charles saw that he was climbing down towards a large group of hostile pikemen and halberdiers.

Worsley and Osborne again realized that something had happened and clattered down the hill with the riderless horse. This time, Hammond had effectively sprung a trap. As they reached the ford at Carisbrooke, they were hit by a volley of musket fire and rode hell for leather towards the waiting ship off Wootton Park. New Model cavalry – Cromwell's Ironsides – were on their trail the whole time.

The ship's master, seeing no king with the fleeing royalists, ordered his crew to row off the beach, leaving the pair to their own devices. When the cavalry arrived, they saw the ship weighing anchor and assumed that the birds had flown. In fact, the pair hid in the woods until the troop wheeled to ride back to Newport.

It is odd that, given Charles' untrustworthy track record, he should be given parole early in September 1648 to attend the Treaty of Newport. He slept in the house of William Hopkins in Holyrood Street, from where he would have been driven by coach, two hundred yards to the old grammar school where the treaty was signed. Both buildings still stand today.

Sir William Hopkins' house in Newport, where King Charles I stayed during the meeting which culminated in the Treaty of Newport, 1648. Carol Trow

Nothing was likely to come of this meeting. It was in no sense a treaty with a binding outcome – merely a reiteration of the demands from parliament made fifteen months before. By now the various risings had been put down and the Scottish threat seriously diminished by Cromwell at the battle of Preston. While both sides argued their case behind the grey stone walls of the school, the national spotlight fell on Newport.

People came from everywhere – soldiers (who had to be paid by extra taxes levied on the town); courtiers, members of parliament; all their servants; hangers-on. What trouble there was centred on the George Inn, in the High Street. On 9 November a running battle lasting half an hour broke out here between cavaliers, armed with rapiers and pistols and musketeers from the castle. There were an unknown number of deaths and the wounded were frog-marched up the hill to Carisbrooke. A large number of women arrived in Newport too, almost certainly prostitutes of various social classes. One of them 'conceitedly deckt with black patches or ambitious spots on her face', made a play for the king himself, but Charles was not interested. He was still very much in love with his wife, Henrietta Maria, despite her enforced absence in France. And anyway, by this time Charles Stuart was already fighting for his life.

This might have gone on for months. The king was a past-master of prevarication and eventually the Army lost patience. Hammond was arrested on 27 November. Three days later, during a downpour, Charles was spirited away through Yarmouth to Hurst Castle. It was the start of the journey that would lead to his eventual execution outside his own palace of Whitehall at the end of January 1649.

'What an Island we had,' wrote Oglander, 'from 1643 till 1650 ... For our Captain we have now a Governor, as if we were slaves.' And his old

'By Appointment' - a seventeenth-century painting on plaster in the upper storey of William Hopkins' house is a reminder of its royal visitor in 1648. Carol Trow with kind permission of Just For You

snobbery shows through with the mention of 'Templar, a collarmaker in Newport whom they made Marshall.'

But the Stuart connection with the Island had not quite come to an end. In August 1650, the two royal children who had not fled overseas were brought to Carisbrooke as prisoners. Henry stayed there until 1653 when Cromwell let him go to rejoin his exiled family. But there was to be no reprieve for Elizabeth. A few days short of her fifteenth birthday, she caught a chill in a rainstorm on the Bowling Green and died, probably of pneumonia, on 8 September 1650. The room where she died can still be seen and her marble tomb stands in St Thomas's Church.

Chapter 7

In Search of Michal Morey

Michal Morey he is dead,
For chopping off his grandson's head.
He is hung on Arreton Down
For rooks and ravens to peck down.

Any crime that becomes a children's rhyme must have something special about it. On the surface, the murder of fourteen-year-old James Dove in woodland below Arreton Down has it all. There are two folkloric versions of the tale. In the first, crabby old Michal Morey, living at Sullens on the slopes of the Downs that overlook Shide and beyond that, Newport, lost his temper with his grandson because the boy was slow in bringing him a meal (breakfast or dinner – the repast varies). Furious, the old man lashed out with the nearest murderous object, a billhook and proceeded to hack the boy to death.

In a panicked attempt to conceal the crime, he burnt the house down (hence the nearest road name, Burnt House Lane) and fled. He got as far as a cave in the chalk quarry at Downend, less than half a mile away and hid there. Despite the hue and cry that was set up for him, local inhabitants and friends left food at the cave's entrance.

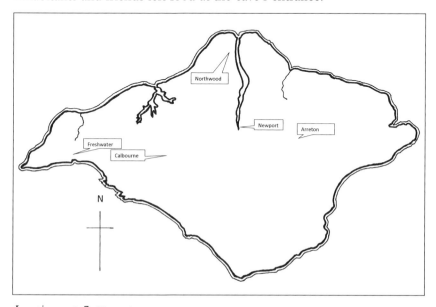

Location map 7. The author

Two versions of Morey's end exist in legend. The local militia from Newport found the cave and killed him, probably with musket fire. Alternatively, he was captured, either by the militia or the hue and cry mob, hustled to the ridge at Arreton and hanged within sight of his crime. Yet a third account follows the latter version but has a kangaroo trial in Newport first.

Almost nothing about this case makes sense. Even the careful research carried out by Kenneth Phillips in 1981 leaves many crucial questions unanswered.

Michal or Micah Morey was baptised in the church at Arreton on 21 April 1672. This was usually done within days of a birth because of the high infant mortality rate at the time. He was the youngest son of Henry Morey and nothing is known about his childhood and young manhood. Michal's first child, Mary, was baptised in the same church on 14 November 1696. It is reasonable to assume that Michal was already well-established as a wood-cutter in the area, and the badly-paid and precarious living did not prevent the family being extended to six by 1720.

The next we hear of Mary is on 7 September 1718 when she married Thomas Dove, from Borthwood. The ceremony took place in Freshwater parish church. Four years later, the young couple were back in Arreton and Mary gave birth to her only child, James. She died, of what cause is unknown, on 13 March 1722, but for unexplained reasons was not buried until the thirty first.

Thomas Dove continued to live with his son and father-in-law at the house at Great Sullens (called Syllons on the map of 1810), a cottage and garden granted by Edward Cheeke of Merstone to the Moreys as early as 1654. It is obvious from the evidence put forward at Michal's trial that the house at Sullens could have been fairly full. At various times in the 1720s and '30s, it housed: Michal (who was almost certainly a widower by this time); Thomas and Mary (until her death in 1722); baby James after 1722; Anne Harvey, Michal's sister-in-law, as well as any other of Michal's five other children who may still have been living at home (effectively, that meant Jeane, Richard and Thomas).

By 1727, Thomas Dove had moved out of Sullens and married Elizabeth Loader of Newport in Northwood parish church. For reasons not explained, Dove left the child James behind. This makes it likely that there was a female occupant at Sullens; James was only five and would need a woman's care.

Nothing is known for the next nine years. And suddenly, on a woodside hill not far from Sullens, violence erupted on an appalling scale. Such details as exist from the events of the time make it clear that Michal and James, now fourteen, went into a wood near Arreton carrying leather panniers. Michal either had his billhook (his stock-in-trade tool) with him or he had left one in the wood on an earlier occasion. There was nothing odd about this. It is unlikely that either man had any formal education and James would have probably learnt woodcraft at his grandfather's knee from about the time his father left.

It is not possible to locate the exact murder site today. The 1730s witnessed the first decade of the century's enclosure movement, which saw woods cleared for arable farming, but even so it is likely that Arreton parish was more heavily wooded than today. It was June 1736 and the lush foliage would have concealed the vicious attack that took place.

There was no indoor killing – and therefore no need to burn down a house to conceal the fact. Burnt House Lane may well take its name from an actual incident, but it has no connection with Michal Morey. Kenneth Phillips suggests that the murder was premeditated – hence the panniers – because Morey hacked off the boy's head with the billhook and proceeded to dismember the corpse. Phillips finds it sinister that Morey wore gloves. Why? A woodcutter would be stupid not to protect his hands in his routine work and it would be another hundred and sixty years before fingerprint evidence could be used against him.

The killing in the wood has all the hallmarks of an unpremeditated attack, making nonsense of the second motive in the folkloric version – that Michal killed the boy for an inheritance he had received or was about to receive. No evidence came to light in this context at all. The deed done, Michal Morey panicked. He cut off the boy's arms and legs and stuffed them as best he could into the panniers. Why? Because a buried body – or body parts – would be scented and dug by foxes and a woodsman would know that. Wrapped in a covering, the scent is reduced so scavengers would be less likely to expose the crime.

The event itself appears in Volume 54 of *The Political State of Great Britain*, published for T Cooper at the Globe in Pater Noster Row, the centre of London's bookselling trade for generations.

'An old fellow of the Isle of Wight was condemned for the murder of his grandson, about 14 years of age. He had bred him up from his cradle; and the child having some way disobliged him he took him out with him one morning about six o'clock in June last, on pretence of going to a market town about seven miles from him to buy necessaries and carried him to a wood and murdered him with a billhook which he had taken with him for that purpose.'

It is this which give the notion of premeditation, but since the *Political State* is clearly wrong about the market town (this has to be Newport, less than two miles away) it can be equally wrong about the 'malice aforethought' behind the killing.

The body of Michael Morey hanging in chains on Arreton Down - 'for rooks and ravens to peck down'. The author

Legend and fact agree that Morey ran, but where to is unknown. Would he have gone back to Sullens without James, with some concocted story he hoped the family might believe? Or, in his panic, did he simply put as much distance as he could between himself and the scene of the crime? The former seems likely, at least for a while, because his story was not believed – 'he was taken up on suspicion; and upon searching a chest belonging to him, his bloody shirt was found.'

Again – more questions than answers. How could Morey have returned home in a bloody shirt without its being noticed and assuming that was possible, why did he not destroy or simply wash the shirt to avoid suspicion?

In the search for Michal Morey, there is no mention of the militia, nor of the cave in the Downend quarry. The Arreton Rate Book which has survived gives us a chronology of sorts, but again, there are loopholes. On 16 July, Richard Morey, Michal's eldest son, was paid 8 shillings 'for keeping his father two weeks'. This takes us back to the beginning of July, days and perhaps weeks after the murder itself. The implication is that Michal was under suspicion of murder, perhaps without being charged and that Richard went surety for him; in other words, the old man was under a kind of house arrest. If this was the case, it did not last – Michal 'absconded himself', possibly for a second time and had to be brought back. He was missing for three days, from 24 to 27 July and the total cost of the hue and cry to Arreton parish was £2 6s 9d. A further 6d was spent 'for crying Michal Morey at Newport' on 1 August.

It is possible that the accused was held in Newport under lock and key, but there was no court in the Island with sufficient jurisdiction to try a capital case and Thomas Small, a neighbour – and presumably a carrier by trade – was paid 1 shilling and 3 pence to take Morey to gaol. He cannot have done this alone, because the Arreton Rate Book for 15 August has a further £1 17s for 'carrying Michal Morey to gaol'. Perhaps Small merely took the man, probably in chains in a cart, to the coast for shipping upriver to Southampton and then by road to Winchester.

The wording in the Rate Book for 16 July is odd – 'Expended in searching after the body of James Dove murdered by Michal Morey'. Since the old man had not confessed and the body had not yet been found, this was either written months later or an illegal assumption had been made by the Overseer of the Poor, James Hills, and his fellow vestrymen of Arreton.

The reward for finding James Dove's body was claimed by Richard Norris who came across the dismembered corpse in the middle of October. Decomposition was very advanced. Today, forensic scientists would be able to pinpoint the date of the murder by the extent of the blow-fly larvae infestation. If the summer of 1736 was unusually hot, then decomposition would have been complete by the end of August. The boy's face was unrecognizable, but his ripped and bloodstained clothes would be identification enough.

Norris hurried to James Hills and a team of men went back to Areton woods. The coroner, Mr Redstone and his bailiff were summoned, presumably from Newport and four men stood guard over the remains until an inquest jury could be assembled. This implies that at least part of the inquest took place at the murder site – otherwise the body parts would presumably have been moved. Norris received a two guinea reward for the shock he had received in the undergrowth and Redstone, the bailiff and the watchers got between them £3 2s 9d.

The Arreton undertakers, Henry Hance and Henry Low collected the panniers and their ghastly contents. Gravedigger William Blake was paid half a crown for 'grave and knell', the solemn death toll that called the parish to the funeral. It was probably a large gathering – only Michal Morey was absent, fretting in the confines of Winchester gaol.

Confusing entries in the Rate Book imply that a bizarre twist now took place. That October, Widow Small was called twice from Calbourne as a witness. Since the Morey's neighbour at Sullens was Thomas Small, it is likely that she had known the family well. Kenneth Philips proffers the not unreasonable hypothesis that the woman was called to identify the dead boy's clothes; she may even have made them herself. The fact that she was called twice suggests that some irregularity occurred. The Rate Book's entry for 19 October reads – 'Paid [to William Blake the sexton] in money for taking up the body and burying it again, 6d.'

A Mrs Stallard and others were also paid 4s 6d 'at ye taking up of ye body after burial etc', but precisely what this entailed we do not know. One possible explanation is that Richard Morey, who seems to have stood by his father through thick and thin, demanded that a further identification be made – hence the exhumation and the return of widow Small.

Four months passed before further action was taken. On Sunday 15 February 1737 the vestrymen of Arreton – Robert Moses, John Joliffe, Henry Roberts, Edward Roach, James Hills, James Bissell, John Urry and Thomas Uxford, all local landowners, moved for a bill of indictment against Michal Morey 'for the supposed murder of James Dove'. At last, the law was being adhered to – Morey must be presumed innocent until proven guilty.

During these months Richard Morey had continued to visit his father in gaol and was reimbursed by the parish, which seems extraordinarily generous whether the old man was guilty or not. 'Garnish Money for his father … in Winton Gaol' amounted to 12s 8d.

The trial opened on Saturday 19 March and closed the same day. The solicitor's name was Williams and he also handled the case of Mary Newman, about which nothing is known. He was paid £6 17s 11¹/₂d, which looks suspiciously like money for old rope. There is no record of a prosecution or defence counsel and Morey was not allowed, under the system at the time, to speak in his own defence. The verdict was a foregone conclusion and the sentence for murder was death.

The courthouse and gaol in Winchester in the 1730s was where the Wetherspoons pub now stands in the High Street. Hangings were of course public, intended as a deterrent for the crowd, but actually entertainment for the mob, baying for blood. The gallows was either near the city's Butter Cross or on the hilltop where the law courts stand today.

We have no idea who hanged Michal Morey. In London, the relatively well-chronicled hangman was John Thrift who travelled to various other parts of the country to 'turn off' various cronies of the highwayman-cum-thug Richard Turpin. He may have hanged Morey, but it is equally likely the work was done by a local man. There is no record of the detail of Morey's death, but hanging was an imprecise science which saw the condemned jerking in agony at the end of a rope for up to twenty minutes, urine and faeces running down their legs. Some hangmen grabbed the twitching feet to speed the process, not just for humanitarian reasons, but because the mob could turn on an unpopular or inept hangman.

The sentence at Winchester included the hanging of Morey's body 'in chains at the Isle of Wight'. The purpose of this was, like public hangings, a deterrent. Morey's body would have been soaked in pitch, a tar-like substance which acted as a preservative so that the ghastly spectacle of a rotting corpse would last longer.

The Rate Book refers to Thomas Jeffery 'for hindrance of time in the Michal Morey case', although no explanation is given. John Phillips however made the gibbet or iron cage in which the body would be hung. There is no incontrovertible evidence but it seems highly likely that the gibbet site was on the Bronze Age tumuli on the ridge of Arreton Down, an area known today as Michal Morey's Hump. Excavations carried out there in 1815 found timber deposits in a hole three feet deep and one foot in diameter, indicating a gibbet post. The excavation also revealed seven human skulls and other bones. Later digs in 1878 and 1933 uncovered two more. These are unlikely to be gibbet fodder, but Bronze Age burials for which the tumuli was first built, with what appears to be an overlay of pagan Saxon bodies from the fifth or sixth century.

Folklore of course could accept none of this. By Morey's day, an obsession with the macabre was growing, fuelled by the printing press and a steady increase in literacy. ''Orrible murder' sold newspapers and public

Memento Morey - the skull of the child-murderer on display in the Hare and Hounds *on Arreton Down, yards from the site of the gibbet on which his body hung in chains.* Carol Trow with kind permission of the management of the Hare and Hounds.

executions and gibbetings merely kept the flames alive. Part of Morey's 'cage' ended up as a pipe-rack in a Newport pub. The oak cross-beam that held the cage and even the skull of Michal Morey are today exhibited in the Hare and Hounds, just yards from the tumuli where the rotting corpse creaked and rattled in the wind; the murder story is painted elegantly on the walls. Ghost stories abound. Anyone could whistle up the spectre of Michal Morey, simply by walking twelve times around the Hump and calling his name three times. Such nonsense is the stuff of folklore and it has very little to do with reality.

So what conclusion can we come to in the murder of James Dove? Kenneth Phillips begins with an assertion that the killing was premeditated and then casts doubt on Morey's guilt. It is true that we know nothing of the goings-on at Sullens and cannot begin to guess at the motivation. What no one has considered is what today would be nearly everyone's first assumption. If a sixty-year-old man and a fourteen-year-old boy go into a wood and the boy is killed, we would automatically assume a sexual motive. Had Michal Morey been abusing the boy – and perhaps others of his family – for years? Criminal psychology was not understood in the mid eighteenth century, hence the folkloric need to create the legacy story. Did the old man try it on once too often in that wood that early June morning in 1736? Did the boy rebuff him and did Morey lose his temper, lashing out fatally?

Memories of Morey – legend has it that this beam in the Hare and Hounds *on Arreton Down formed part of the gibbet on which the murderer hung in chains.* Carol Trow with kind permission of the management of the Hare and Hounds

Everything that took place afterwards smacks of panic, the work of a confused, disorganised murderer – perhaps even implying mental illness. Morey did not hide the body well enough; he did not dispose of the blood-stained shirt; he had no plausible story for the boy's disappearance; he ran.

Will we ever know the truth in the search for Michal Morey? Only, perhaps, if we wander the Hump at midnight, circling the ancient mound and whisper his name. Perhaps, then, we can ask him.

Chapter 8

Tom Boulter the Highwayman

The most over-romanticized crime of the eighteenth century was highway robbery, with its image of the 'knight of the road', mounted on a magnificent horse holding up the mail coach with a pair of pistols and the infamous cry, 'Stand and deliver!' Its heroes are Claude Duval, 'the ladies' joy, the ladies' grief'; 'Sixteen String' Jack Rann and above all, Dick Turpin. The false image of highwaymen can be attributed particularly to nineteenth-century novelist Harrison Ainsworth. The real Turpin was a deeply unpleasant, psychotic thug.

The Isle of Wight did not lend itself to highway robbery of this kind. There were certainly wealthy gentlemen, like the Worsleys at Appuldurcombe, the Oglanders at Nunwell, the Campbells at Gatcombe, the Delgarnos at Wolverton and so on. By the middle of the century they represented 'new' money rather than old pedigree; Thomas Dickinson living at Bagwich was a merchant, Henry Roberts at Standen a banker. The richest of these men had property elsewhere – in the case of the Worsleys a 'town house' in London – and they had the habit of carrying

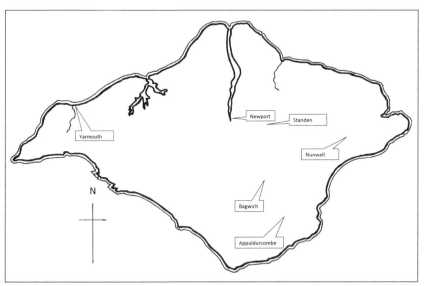

Location map 8. The author

valuables with them by coach between these properties. Even so, the Island was small and most of its roads still dirt tracks. The major route from Newport to Yarmouth (ten miles) had fifty-two gates and carriages usually had a little boy servant on board to open and close these as the carriage passed.

It was easier for highwaymen to hit travellers near major cities, especially London, where the wide-open spaces of Hounslow and Hampstead Heath provided cover from trees and bushes and permitted a fast getaway. The last was vital. Galloping across county boundaries was no problem at all; finding a boat to cross the Solent far more difficult.

To overcome this problem, Thomas Boulter assumed a double identity. By day, he was a respectable citizen of Newport, Isle of Wight. By night he robbed genuinely respectable citizens elsewhere.

Boulter was not an Islander. His family came from Lavington in Wiltshire and seem to have been a fairly disreputable lot. His father was a grist miller at Poulshot near Devizes and he was sent to the local Bridewell (gaol) and whipped in the town's market place for stealing honey from an old woman. Undeterred by the experience, miller Boulton stole a horse from a Mr Hall of Trowbridge and rode it to Andover, where he sold it for £6 (in the 1770s, not a bad price). Caught and sentenced to death – an example of how bloody the Bloody Code was – various friends interceded on his behalf and the sentence was commuted at Winchester to transportation for fourteen years. The likelihood is he never saw home again.

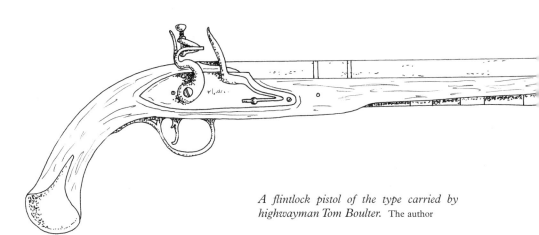

A flintlock pistol of the type carried by highwayman Tom Boulter. The author

Boulter's uncle may well have been the role model for young Tom, born at Poulshot in 1748 or 1750. Outwardly an honest labourer, Isaac Blagden was actually a highwayman until he chose the wrong victim in Colonel Hanger, a gentleman travelling near Market Lavington. The Colonel put two 'slugs' into his thigh and left him bleeding in the road. Pistols in this period fired single shots, so clearly Hanger was more than ready for his man. Luckily for Blagden, he was found and carried to Lavington where a surgeon saved his life. Even so, the man was permanently crippled and spent the rest of his days in the workhouse.

Boulter's mother may have been a criminal too. There is no hard evidence, but she may have been whipped in Devizes market, a punishment usually reserved for thieves and prostitutes. If this was so, James Waylen, writing a history of Devizes in 1859, gives a reason for the subsequent career of little Tom – 'The son who had witnessed the degradation of his mother ever afterwards carried in his heart a motive prompting him to wage war on that society which had countenanced so revolting an outrage.'

Young Tom's education was probably scanty and like most boys he was trained to follow his father's (legal) occupation as a miller. In 1774, the young man may have had a falling out with his father (who received the honey-stealing sentence the following year) and moved to Newport where his sister had opened a milliner's shop. There are no street directories available as early as this, so we have no idea exactly where the shop was. Boulter himself set up as a general grocer in the same premises. We know from personal reminiscences when Waylen wrote that the young grocer dressed fashionably, in a light-coloured coat, red waistcoat and buckskin breeches.

He spent a year in Newport, but during that time bought a brace of pistols and in 1775 visited his mother in Poulshot. This may have been a front. It was, after all, the year in which his father went down, but this is probably a red herring. *Something* however had prodded him into action. Was it, as Waylen suggests 'the routine of a retail business', his 'single year's confinement' in the Isle of Wight? He hired a horse from Mr Cox of the Vine Inn in Southampton and took the Salisbury Road. At Millbrook he rode across country to join the Great Western road between Stockbridge and Sutton.

In less than fifteen minutes, his target approached – the Diligence, clattering towards Salisbury with two passengers. At first, Boulter dithered, riding past the coach two or three times. Finally, he plucked up courage, aimed his pistols at the driver and robbed the passengers of their watches and money, thanking them and explaining that he was strapped for cash. Buoyed up by the ease of all this, he doubled back via another route to Salisbury, robbing five more travellers on the Plain before reaching Poulshot. He now had seven watches and perhaps £40 in coins and notes.

Having spent some time with his mother, Boulter took the turnpike road towards Andover and robbed a post-chaise, several horsemen and three men on foot returning from market. At Andover, he dined (presumably very well) at the Swan and made his way to Winchester, robbing another chaise on the Basingstoke turnpike. Then he caught the first packet from Southampton to the Island.

Waylen ignores the passage of time, but it is likely that Boulter's first highway robbery outing took two days, not one and that he stayed overnight with his mother. As far as anyone in Newport knew, the grocer had merely gone to visit family. They were unaware of the loot in his luggage or the pistols probably hidden in the lining of his coat.

For the next few months, Boulter repeated the exercise. Targeting the roads he knew well, 'the flying highwayman of Wiltshire' had the perfect bolt-hole to retreat to, where, presumably, his sister would cover for him and provide alibis.

By 1777, Boulter believed, probably rightly, that the south was too hot for him, so he went north. Now however, he was on unfamiliar ground and picked on the wrong targets near Ripon when a gentleman and his servant managed to disarm him. He was convicted of attempted highway robbery at the York Assizes and he was sentenced to death. A reprieve came through at the last minute and he was sent to the Army instead. 'Poore', the nickname he had given himself on the road, could not have been given this alternative at a worse time. Raw recruits as well as experienced men were being drafted to America in ever increasing numbers to put down the rebellion in the Thirteen Colonies. Perhaps this, or the rigours of army life didn't appeal remotely to Boulter and he ran south again. Now, he could add 'army deserter' to his criminal vitae.

At Bristol, Boulter teamed up with James Caldwell of the Ship Inn in Milk Street. There was now a reward of £40 on his head, but his front in the Island was so secure that no one knew where his base was. One of his victims however was out for revenge.

Thomas Fowle of Devizes had been robbed by two men near the Eleven Mile Stone out of Salisbury. In advertisements he placed in as many papers as he could find, Fowle described his watch and gave descriptions of his attackers. Both rode dark brown horses, one with white heels and they wore surtouts, the traditional long overcoats used for riding. One of them was over 5ft 10, a little taller than average and Fowle offered a personal reward for £40 for their capture.

The journalist in the paper that carried this advertisement on Christmas Eve 1777 clearly had further information, because Boulter was named as having attacked a Mr Bayly of Devizes earlier the same day, 'in company with an assistant, a desperate villain'. An hour after they relieved Fowle of his watch and five guineas the pair held up Mr Bennett, a Langford farmer going to Hilcot with one of his labourers, Thomas Chink. Bennett gave up his eight guineas in gold and one shilling of silver, but when Chink only gave them six shillings, he was butt-whipped by one of them and his pockets ransacked to the tune of three guineas.

The robbing spree continued for the rest of the day. In the darkness of the evening, Mr Cook was deprived of £10 on the road to Seend. A farmer lost his watch and a servant coughed up about 40 shillings belonging to his master, Mr Anstie. Somebody, though, fought back. A butcher was knocked off his horse but parried several cutlass slashes with an 'iron weapon' and scrambled away through a hedge with pistol balls whizzing round him.

'It is astonishing,' ranted the Salisbury Journal, 'that such a villain as Boulter should so long escape the hands of justice.' The description of him was useless however – 'about five feet seven inches high, brown hair, a well-looking man, about 28 years of age, by trade a miller, living lately at Poulshot'. What it did not say, of course, was that he was still living at Newport, Isle of Wight!

Fowle's fury led to further articles in the days that followed. Over and above the £40 reward provided by the government, a further 30 guineas was offered for Boulter and ten for his accomplice, to be lodged at the bank in Devizes on conviction. Confusingly however, Boulter had now grown three inches and was 'stout made' with light hair and a crooked nose. His accomplice was five feet nine, 'thin made', about twenty five and had long black hair.

Boulter's reign of terror came to an end in Birmingham the following year. A Jewish 'fence' probably preferred the reward to the watch the pair offered him and they were imprisoned. True to his slippery reputation, however, Boulter managed to dig his way out (literally) through the wall of his cell in Clerkenwell gaol and drop down into the street. This was not too surprising, although the place had been rebuilt between 1774 and '75. It was described as 'a great brothel, kept under the protection of the law for the emolument of its ministers.' Jack Sheppard, an even more notorious felon than Boulter, had escaped from Clerkenwell, along with his mistress, the rather large Edgeworth Bess; but then, there were few places that could hold Sheppard for long.

Boulter made for the coast, not this time to his safe haven in the Island, but to Bridport in Dorset. Perhaps his cover had been blown and he was making for France. Whatever the reason, he was captured, tried and executed along with Caldwell at Winchester on 19 August 1778.

Chapter 9

The Governor's Wife
or Sir Richard Worse-Than-Sly

Today, the strikingly handsome Richard Worsley is best remembered for a monumental four hundred page *History of the Isle of Wight*. It appeared in June 1781. The *London Monthly Review* was ecstatic – 'so well written and so respectably authenticated'. Others were less sure. That well-known gossip and all round bitch, Horace Walpole wrote 'I have gone through Sir R Worsley's Isle of Wight, which is in my own way – and yet alas! I did not find one diamond in that dunghill.' He noticed that Worsley had dedicated the book to the king (the already ailing George III) and had the man down for a crawler. He would no doubt have been delighted by the bizarre events of the following year.

Worsley was a Baronet, Comptroller of the king's household and a member of the Privy Council. But at a local level, he was Governor of the Island and lived in a magnificent, now partially ruined, house at Appuldurcombe, near Ventnor. He was also a colonel in the Hampshire Militia and the newly-appointed captain of the sixty-strong Isle of Wight

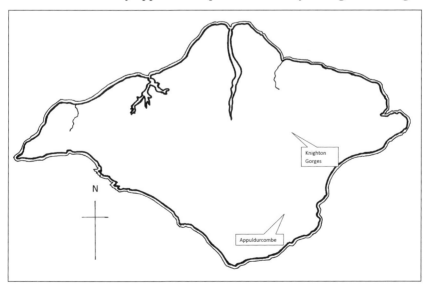

Location map 1. The author

In the KING BENCH, Westminster-Hal

Sir Richard and Lady Seymour Worsley, whose antics shocked Georgian society. The author

Company was George Maurice Bisset who had recently bought the Dillington family home at Knighton Gorges. The two men were friends – in fact, it was Worsley who had given Bisset the appointment, but the lurid events which took place at Maidstone changed all that for ever.

On 15 September 1775, Worsley, worth about £5000 a year, married the daughter of Sir John Fleming. Since Sir John was dead, the new bride was worth about £70,000 (some said £80,000) and on marriage, the fortune came Worsley's way. The oddly named Seymour Worsley, nee Fleming, was a striking beauty, famous in polite society for being a flirt. Just how much of a flirt came to a head in 1782 when Worsley took Bisset to court on a charge of 'criminal conversation' with Lady Worsley.

The subsequent scandal was perhaps escapism at a grim time for the country. Throughout the years of the Worsley's marriage, which produced two children and probably an awful lot of rows, the War of American Independence was fought and lost. Although formalities limped on until 1783, General Cornwallis's surrender at Yorktown two years earlier was effectively the end. At home, on a personal note of immorality, George, Prince of Wales set up his own court, where he attracted men like himself, who put women, gambling and the high life before anything else.

Seen in this context, the rather grubby goings on of Lady Worsley seem almost to be expected. Joshua Reynolds painted her in a magnificent scarlet militia uniform, complete with blue facings and silver lace. Her accompanying her husband on war game manoeuvres in Sussex and Kent struck some as splendidly patriotic and loving; others as scandalous. A lady had no place in an army camp, even an amateur one like the militia; but it did give the man-hungry Seymour a chance to meet a lot of dashing officers.

Eventually, Worsley cracked. No doubt realizing there was money to be made out of his wife's infidelity, he brought the charge against Bisset in February 1782 at the King's Bench in Westminster, demanding damages of £20,000 on the grounds that Bisset 'debauched, deflowered, lay with and carnally knew' his wife. Laying aside the technical nonsense of deflowering – Seymour was a married woman, mother of two and was reputed to have gone through twenty seven lovers – here was a marvellous opportunity for the scandal sheets of the day to make a great deal of capital.

The judge, that grey February day in Westminster Hall, was a towering figure of jurisprudence, one of the most terrifying judges of the day; William, Earl Mansfield. The man's judgements were usually fair, but he had a reputation as a hanging judge and the mob had burned his house down during the Gordon Riots two years earlier.

The jury, whose names have survived, were, of course, all male, gentlemen living in Westminster. For his counsel, Worsley could afford the Attorney General and three junior barristers, Lee, Dunning and Erskine. Bisset, almost certainly on a smaller income, fielded three – Bearcroft, Howarth and Pechell.

The first witness was Captain Leversage, an officer in the Hampshire Militia who recalled a social gathering at his house in Lewes. The Worsleys were invited, but Lady Worsley arrived alone, her husband sending a message to say he was not very well. At a quarter past one in the morning, Lady Worsley left in the company of Captain Bisset, Leversage no doubt supposing he would see her home.

Three or four hours later, Leversage was woken up by a frantic thumping on his front door. First one of Worsley's servants, then Worsley himself turned up, demanding to know where Lady Worsley was.

The servant was Francis Godfrey and he was the court's next witness. In fact he had only been in Worsley's employ for one day and now found himself in at the deep end in a very messy situation. Godfrey sat up until the early hours, waiting for his mistress' return. Then the colonel, 'much agitated' had sent him to Leversage's and obviously decided to follow hard on his heels.

The party had taken place on Sunday 18 November and although the transcript of the trial is confusing, it appears that Bisset took Lady Worsley to his lodgings where his landlord, Mr Stubbs, heard suspicious comings and goings in the small hours. Stubbs didn't see anybody, but heard someone other than Bisset go down the stairs and the clatter of hoofs as a chaise drove off over the cobbles below his window.

The pair clearly made for London, because the next morning Thomas Bourn, a waiter at the Royal Hotel in Pall Mall let a 'lady and gentleman' into the Apollo drawing room a little after two o'clock. This time-lag is explained by the appalling roads of the day. Turnpike trusts had been set up to charge travellers tolls for road repair, but these in themselves slowed travel down and entire stretches of road were not covered by the Trusts, so the surface, especially in late autumn, was a nightmare. Having served the pair breakfast, Bourn then lit a fire in Room 14. At this point, Lord Mansfield, anxious to be fair, interrupted to ask Bourn how he knew the pair actually went to bed. The waiter had to concede, he couldn't be certain.

For the next four or five days, Bisset and Lady Worsley stayed at the Royal to all intents and purposes as man and wife. Ann Watkinson, housekeeper at the hotel, no doubt raised a ribald titter in court when asked what was the distinction between sleeping and lying in a room. 'I did not see them sleep,' she answered. She and Mrs Commande, another servant, had both seen the pair in bed together.

At the close of the Plaintiff's evidence, Worsley must have felt rather smug, especially when Bisset's counsel, Bearcroft, did not seriously challenge the fact that his client had behaved adulterously with Lady Worsley. His smugness did not last long however, because Bearcroft had not one, but several, aces up his sleeve.

First he produced Mary Marriott, a maid at a bathing establishment near Maidstone, where the Worsleys owned property. The previous September 'at the latter end of the hop-season' Lady Worsley took a cold bath and went into a corner to dress. At that point, a face appeared at the small window overhead – it was George Bisset. At the same time, Richard Worsley called out, 'Seymour! Seymour! Bisset is going to get up to look at you.' Bisset stayed there for about five minutes, during which time, Lady Worsley leisurely dressed and joined Bisset and Worsley outside. It was clear from Marriott's testimony that Bisset could not have reached the window without some sort of assistance from Worsley, 'and that Sir Richard might easily have pulled him down if he pleased.' All three of them went off, laughing and joking.

Next in the list of Bearcroft's damned was Lord Deerhurst who first met Lady Worsley in 1779. Asked what he thought of her character, he replied,

'I thought her very dissolute and that she was unfaithful to her husband.' Pressed as to Worsley's attitude to his wife's behaviour, Deerhurst, apparently affronted, said, 'I hope I am not called to betray any private conversation?'

The judge assured him he was not, but Deerhurst proceeded to spill the beans anyway. 'He [Worsley] did then say that many young men had tried her, to no effect and that I had his permission to try my chance with her. But he said it jokingly ...'

Deerhurst had spent ten days at Appuldurcombe in the Island in September and admitted in court that Worsley had caught him in his wife's dressing room, next to her bedroom, at four in the morning. Deerhurst couldn't remember whether Lady Worsley was dressed then or not. Worsley said to him, 'Deerhurst, how came you here?' but since the guest stayed for four more days and accompanied Lady Worsley to a party in Southampton, it appeared the host was not much perturbed.

Asked if he was intimate with Lady Worsley on a trip to Godalming, Deerhurst declined to answer. Mansfield backed him up, no doubt with a withering glance at counsel. 'Certainly – you have no right to be asked that.' The jury of course, were busy drawing their own conclusions, especially when Deerhurst told them that two other men chaperoned Lady Worsley and again there was no objection from Sir Richard.

Lord Peterborough, the next witness, had met Lady Worsley in the spring of 1780. He remembered it clearly because it was the seasonal opening of the London pleasure ground known as Ranelagh, where music, dancing and assignations were the order of the day. He had, in fact, first met Seymour at Sadler's Wells – all of this part of the fashionable London circuit for the aristocracy and gentry. He did not believe that Lady Worsley 'conducted herself as a decent, modest wife', but gave no details.

Bourchier Smith, recalling an outing on Shooters Hill, painted a picture of a husband and wife going their own way. Worsley drove off 'to town' in his phaeton, leaving his wife in the company of others.

The Marquis of Graham visited the Worsleys and found her 'gay, lively and free' in her behaviour. She was not immodest however and there was no 'absolute impropriety in her conduct', leaving the jury to ponder how much the Marquis had not said in his time in the witness box.

The most appalling evidence, however, about which Lord Mansfield was furious, came from Dr Osborne, who attended Lady Worsley at their London home. Osborne began with a proper regard for doctor-patient privilege 'but I have the lady's permission to give evidence of the truth.' Having loftily said 'My business was to cure her; and I do not choose to talk upon the subject..' he had already told the court that Lady Worsley 'had some complaints on her, which I fancy were the consequence of a Venereal Disorder'.

Despite a rather belated effort by Worsley's counsel to counter the most damning evidence – the spying in the bath story – the damage was done. According to Mr J Fraser, the window in the bath-house was only chest high; in other words, Bisset could have peered in without the connivance of Worsley.

Mansfield's summation was very fair. He pointed out that there was no contestation of the fact that Bisset and Lady Worsley were guilty of adultery. The issue turned on the size of damages that should be awarded to Sir Richard. 'This woman,' said Mansfield, 'for three or four years, has been prostituted with a variety of people – that is extremely clear.' He then went on to point out how odd it was that Worsley offered his wife to Lord Deerhurst, albeit in jest and didn't seem to mind finding the man in his wife's dressing room in the early hours of the morning. 'If you think the husband was privy to, consenting and encouraging this debauchery, he ought not to have your verdict.'

The jury retired for less than an hour and returned to find for the Plaintiff; in other words, Worsley had won. The kick in the teeth however, was that rather than the £20,000 Worsley had demanded from Bisset, he was awarded 1 shilling!

What are we to make of the handsome colonel of militia, Governor of the Island, historian and benefactor of the poor? Some would say he was indifferent to his wife, with interests elsewhere. But the evidence of the trial paints a different picture. He comes across as a rather weird figure, almost pimping for his wife who seemed to enjoy every minute of it. There is something disturbingly voyeuristic about the bath incident.

That, certainly, is how the satirical cartoonist James Gilray saw it. On 14 March 1782 his 'Sir Richard Worse-than-sly, exposing his wife's bottom – o fye!' caused a sensation and London's polite society rushed to buy a copy. It seems to be taken straight from the trial transcript. Mary Marriott stands by, holding her ladyship's clothes while Seymour herself is standing naked, up to her ankles in the bath. George Bisset, in his militia uniform, is leering at her through the open window, sitting on the shoulders of a happily accommodating Richard Worsley.

Worsley's career was over. London society enjoyed it all enormously, but the Worsleys were a laughing stock. Even so, it took the Governor six years to separate from Seymour. George Bisset took the whole thing very badly. He had already resigned his commission in the Isle of Wight militia and perhaps had some hope of Seymour Worsley actually going through with what appeared to be an elopement via the Royal Hotel. In that, he was to be disappointed. Having paid Worsley his shilling, he retired to his Island home at Knighton Gorges, ostracized by the local gentry. Rumour had it that Bissett had set up a watered-down version of Francis Dashwood's notorious Hellfire Club at the house, where women and wine were available in plentiful measure. Among his guests, allegedly, were the actor David Garrick and the polemist John Wilkes, a member of the actual Hellfire Club who had a house at nearby Sandown.

Abandoning Knighton Gorges, Bissett lived out his years as a recluse in a gardener's cottage on the estate, dying, it was said, of tertiary syphilis given to him by Lady Worsley. Before he died, he ordered the destruction of Knighton Gorges stone by stone. Today, only the gateposts remain, amid tales of haunting and the sad music of parties, long gone.

Chapter 10

The Loss of the
Royal George

Six months after the Worsley-Bisset humiliation in the high court, a far worse disaster struck an estimated eight hundred people on board the navy's flagship, the *Royal George*. In an incident which has echoes of the *Mary Rose*, the sinking of the most famous British ship afloat sent shock-waves through the naval establishment and the country in general and should never have happened.

In 1746, the navy embarked on a ten-year build of the *Royal Anne*, subsequently renamed the *Royal George* to be the biggest ship in the service. Her deck was more than 200 feet long and fifty feet wide. She weighed 3745 tons and her three decks carried one hundred guns. It took an astonishing 100,000 cubic feet of finest oak and elm to build her and she had a top speed of 11 knots.

The *George* gained rapid honours in the Seven Years War (1756-63) sinking two French warships at Quiberon Bay during a gale. The French flagship, the *Soleil Royale* was ablaze already from the *George*'s guns

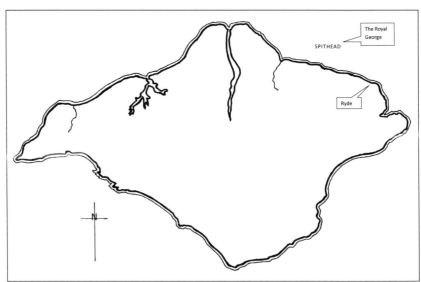

Location map 10. The author

when the 70 gun *Superbe* came to her rescue. A single devastating broadside at point blank range sent the Frenchman to the bottom with huge loss of life.

In the years between the Seven Years War and the War of American Independence, the *George* was effectively in mothballs in Plymouth. Those were embarrassing years for the navy. Having weathered the execution of Admiral Byng for cowardice in the face of the enemy, successive penny-pinching senior officers at the Admiralty Board had let the bulk of the fleet fall into a state of neglect. When a Franco-Spanish fleet supporting the American colonists sailed into the Channel in 1779, the *George* had to turn tail. Bewildered crewmen with tears in their eyes, stripped off their jackets and tied them over the wooden eyes of their figurehead, so that it at least could not witness the disgrace. In the following year, however, the *George* captured two Spanish warships off Portugal and salvaged something of her honour.

In the summer of 1782, having just undergone a refit, she joined the rest of the fleet anchored at Spithead, ready to sail to the relief of Gibraltar. The Solent in the eighteenth century often bristled with the masts and spars of warships, but that August was exceptional. There were more than fifty men-of-war, including the yet-to-be-famous *Victory* and between two and three hundred merchant ships and boats, ferrying supplies in all directions for the largest armada ever to leave England.

The chain of command on the *George* was complicated by the fact that, as a flagship, it carried the senior admiral commanding, Richard Kempenfelt, a sixty-four-year-old veteran of East India campaigns and the Seven Years War. Promoted to rear-admiral two years earlier, he had won a spectacular victory off Ushant in 1781 and had a reputation of a very able, far-seeing man. His ideas of health in the seething hell-holes that were the navy's ships were far ahead of his time and his organizational systems remained in use in the British navy until the twentieth century.

In all operational matters on the *George* however, the man giving the orders was Captain Martin Waghorn and he inexplicably ordered the ship to careen (be tilted in the water) so that repairs could be made to a water cock below the water-line. Ships like the *George* were built of oak, but their hulls were sheathed in copper to prevent barnacle encrustation. It was the job of the ship's carpenter to check the timbers every day to look for signs of wear or stress and among the *George*'s supplies would be a stock of timber for the purpose.

Waghorn's decision was odd to say the least. 'Heeling' a ship as loaded as the *George* was, with 548 tons of supplies and 83 tons of ammunition would be an ambitious task, but on 29 August it was probably impossible.

The crew, including all but Kempenfelt, mustered 820 men. This included a company of scarlet-coated marines under a captain whose job it was to provide small-arms fire when the *George* came alongside an enemy ship. But there were an estimated 360 civilians on board that day too, arriving on over-crowded bumboats from Portsmouth harbour and perhaps the Island. A percentage of the *George*'s crew, like that of any warship, was made of pressed men, victims of the notorious Press Gangs that haunted the smoky taverns of seaports and docks in search of 'likely lads'. Such were conditions on board a man-of-war that even volunteers were likely to desert on reaching land. For that reason, no shore leave was granted for the ordinary seamen and all the pleasures of home were shipped out to the waiting men.

The *George*, then, on that August day, was hopelessly overcrowded. Nearly twelve hundred people jostled on its decks and galleys – wives and sweethearts bidding their loved ones farewell; children saying goodbye to their fathers. Hawkers and tinkers did a roaring trade in keepsakes and prostitutes plied their trade too, perhaps between the guns where there was a modicum of privacy.

In this carnival mayhem, the marines beat to quarters at 7.20 in the morning. The carpenter and his team were lowered over the starboard side on a platform and the cannon were manoeuvred into position to shift its weight and make it tilt. No one seems to have been in overall charge of these operations. Despite the ban on shore leave, the Master, the Bosun and the Gunner, three vital specialists, were somewhere in Portsmouth, unaware that all Hell was about to break loose.

With the portside gun ports open and just a foot above the water-line, supplies were still being passed in that way. There was no wind, but at Spithead there is a double flood tide which makes the sea choppy even in calm weather and by nine o'clock, a serious amount of water was splashing into holds, bilges and the lower gundeck.

About this time, a fifty-ton cutter, *The Lark*, arrived alongside with barrels of rum, the 'grog' that was routinely doled out to sailors twice a day. The extra weight that all this created saw the *George* slip lower into the water. Her top mast and spars were now at an alarming angle and the ship's carpenter knew it was time to act. He fought his way through the crowds, still merry-making, to the knot of officers on the quarter-deck.

In the heated confrontation that followed, Lieutenant Hollingsbury sent the man below. At first, mindful no doubt of the vast gulf that existed between officers and men and the navy's ready use of the lash, the carpenter obeyed. He was back in minutes, however and this time Hollingsbury yelled at him, 'Damn you, sir! If you can run the ship better than I you had better take command.' Better indeed – and for everyone on board.

Bobbing back in a boat on his way to the *George*, the Master realized the danger. The *George* had been slowly sinking for twenty minutes by the time the carpenter finally got to Waghorn, and by then it was too late. To their horror, the team on the platform on the starboard side saw the ship rise out of the water, her barnacle-crusted copper keel like a giant whale rolling over.

Waghorn's frantic orders to right the ship saw hundreds of sailors tumbling down to the lower decks to haul at the guns. The angle was now too steep for them and many were thrown into the surging sea, only to have the *George*'s 3745 tons plus cargo, guns and people, roll over them. There was now panic everywhere. Most sailors of Kempenfelt's day could not swim and those who could were being pulled down by the majority. Kempenfelt's cabin door was jammed and we have no idea why he did not react to events. Even if he was busy with charts and battle-plans, the sliding of ink-wells, paper and other paraphernalia must have alerted him to the problem. Had he, perhaps, been knocked out by falling timbers? Or suffered a heart attack? We shall never know. Some officers tore off their heavy, braided coats before diving from the rolling timbers. One who survived was Lieutenant Durham, a Scot from Largo in Fife. 'The men caught hold of each other 30 or 40 at a time,' he told the subsequent court martial, 'and drowned one another.' A panicking marine pulled Durham underwater twice before the navy man was able to tear off his waistcoat and swim clear. When the marine's body floated to the surface two weeks later, Durham's waistcoat was still tangled in his arms.

Surrounded though she was by potential help, the *George* went down quickly. The horror-struck companies of neighbouring ships put out their boats at once and picked up perhaps three hundred survivors. One of these was a small boy, clinging to a live sheep that had been part of the George's stores and was instinctively swimming out of danger. The shocked child could not remember his name, so his rescuers called him John Lamb.

The ship's Master must have regretted his visit to Portsmouth, but still more perhaps, his return. He went down with the *George*, as did the carpenter and Admiral Kempenfelt.

> But Kempenfelt is gone,
> His victories are o'er,
> And he and his eight hundred
> Shall plough the waves no more.

– wrote the poet, W Cowper. But if England felt the loss, the navy was anxious to cover up a disaster of its own making.

As the bodies washed ashore in Portsmouth and on the north coast of the Island, a ship's surgeon wrote, 'Portsmouth and Gosport were in a state of commotion. Almost everyone had lost some relation, friend or acquaintance. Every hour corpses were coming ashore on the beach. Every hour the bell was tolling and the long procession winding through the streets.'

There had to be an enquiry, but the navy was in no mood to blame its officers, whose fault the loss of the *Royal George* blatantly was. Five admirals sat in judgement in the captain's day quarters on the Warspite, all powdered wigs and gold lace, Waghorn's sword on the table before them. It is unlikely any of them had much respect for Waghorn *per se*, but he was the symbol of authority and control in the navy – Admiral Kempenfelt even more so. If men like this could not be trusted, then what hope had Britain of holding its colonies together, much less obtain command of the seas? The blame was shifted to the Navy Board, the dockyard authority composed largely of civilians.

Seizing on the evidence of two of the thirteen witnesses they called, the Admirals noted a shipwright who claimed that some of the *George*'s timbers were rotten and a long-serving gunner who swore he heard a 'bodily crack' as the ship heeled to. It is true that neglect had been the order of the day for years, with laxity and embezzlement proving obstacles to efficiency. The *George*, however, had just put to sea after a refit, so it is unlikely she was that rotten.

Waghorn's sword was returned to him. Hollingsbury, whose arrogance had contributed massively to the disaster, was not only acquitted of all blame, but rose to become a ship's captain in his own right.

For sixty years, the *Royal George* sat at the bottom of the Solent, her topmasts visible above the water line, a navigational hazard for pilots weaving their way around her. William Tracey put forward a plan to raise her in the months following the sinking, but the Navy Board, convinced of its own guilt, made it impossible for him through a lack of co-operation. Not until 1839 did Colonel Palsey, a pioneer in deep-water diving, lift the remaining cannon and destroy the *George* with gunpowder. By that time, the ship and her guns were obsolete; the last naval battle using sail was fought off Navarino Bay against the Turks in 1827. The melted bronze was used to build the great memorial to Nelson in Trafalgar Square.

A number of stone tablets were erected to the dead of 29 August. One, in St Mary's church, Portsmouth read, 'A Testimony of Sympathy for the Unfortunates who perished by the sinking of the HMS *Royal George* ... Erected by one who was a stranger both to officers and the ship's company.' The use of the word 'unfortunates' is very telling. It does not merely mean all those who drowned, but specifically the scores of prostitutes on board at the time.

In the 1840s, property developers working on Ryde's Eastern Esplanade uncovered skeletons laid out side by side in a mass grave. More came to light in the 1930s when the Canoe Lake was dug. They were the drowned of the *Royal George* and a memorial was officially unveiled to them by Lord Louis Mountbatten, then Governor of the Island, in 1965. A further service was held in 2006 when the memorial was moved slightly further inland.

How many Islanders died that August day we cannot know. The navy buried its mistakes and let the sea roll over them.

Chapter 11

Watching the Wall

Them that asks no questions
Isn't told a lie.
Watch the wall, my darling,
While the Gentlemen go by.

'A Smuggler's Song'
Rudyard Kipling

There are two crimes that have been hijacked by mythmakers – robbery committed on the 'high Toby' by 'knights of the road' (see Chapter 8) and smuggling. Every book ever written on the latter contains the Kipling poem quoted above as well as romantic tales of secret caves, mysterious lights on dark clifftops and supernatural goings-on.

The reality is rather more prosaic and the widespread involvement of maritime communities like the Isle of Wight made it almost impossible for the authorities to cope. At the same time, accurate research is made all the more difficult by a folkloric approach to the subject which is thin on details of time and place.

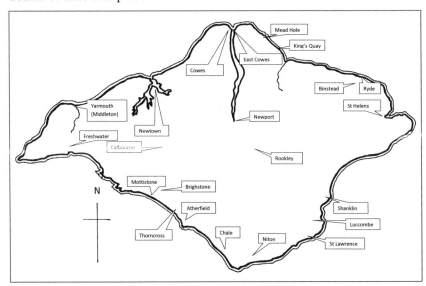

Location map 11. The author

The cliffs at the 'back o' the Wight', notorious haunt of smugglers in the eighteenth century. Carol Trow

Mead Hole, the pirate lair on the Island's North-East coast, continued as a haven for smuggled goods long after the days of piracy. King's Quay, a small inlet further along the coast towards Wootton, played its part in this respect too.

What transformed the 'secret economy' of the Island was the growing obsession of successive eighteenth-century governments to increase their revenue by levying prohibitive duties on imported goods. In this way, tea, coffee, chocolate and sugar remained gentlemen's luxury goods for most of the century. Dr Samuel Johnson, compiling the country's first dictionary, defined a smuggler as 'a wretch who, in defiance of the law, imports and exports goods without the payment of customs.' Adam Smith, progenitor of free trade, wrote in *The Wealth of Nations* in 1776 – 'A Smuggler is a person who, no doubt blameable for violating the laws of his country, is frequently incapable of violating those of natural justice and would have been in every respect an excellent citizen had not the laws of his country made that a crime that nature never meant to be so.'

The Prime Minister William Pitt was the first politician brave enough to put the theorist Smith's ideas into practice by slashing duties on goods. In 1784 that on tea fell from 117% to 12½%; overnight, tea became the drink of the working class.

Before that however – and for many years afterwards – the avoidance of any duty at all became a way of life for Islanders. Rather like today's drugs trade, it flourished not just because of the smugglers/dealers themselves, but because there was a large and ready market for the goods concerned. When Commander C Deare of the Royal Navy wrote a report on the extent of smuggling in the Island in 1836, he said - 'I have been told (and such is the demoralised condition of the inhabitants that I believe it) that 8 out of 10 of the whole population are consumers of contraband spirits, tobacco and tea and they consider ... there is no harm in it.'

That was precisely the problem. Like that other old country pastime, poaching, smuggling was a social crime – the only victim was the government, remote, unfeeling and greedy. Today, when revenue is returned to the country via roads, schools, the health service and the police, we can all see a point to the imposition of taxes. In the heyday of smuggling, the government only spent money on defence – there was no effective feedback to the men of the Wight.

Kipling's poem famously refers to 'brandy for the parson, baccy for the clerk, laces for a lady, letters for a spy', but this only ruffles the surface of the list of contraband. Coconut shells, gold and silver brocade, ribbons, girdles, chocolate or cocoa paste, calico, gloves, silk; Persian, Chinese or East India textiles – all these and more were specifically the trinkets of the rich. It was not *too* surprising then that when exciseman Thomas Fisher and his nine-man team arrested a smuggling crew coming ashore at midnight at Shanklin on 9 August 1744, the leader of the gang upbraided him and threatened him with dismissal. The leader was J Popham of Shanklin and he was a Justice of the Peace. As if to illustrate Commander Deare's view of the vast numbers involved in illegal 'freetrading' a century later, a crowd of locals appeared from nowhere on the clifftops and began hurling stones at the excisemen.

The Isle of Wight was a poor relation in terms of smuggling by comparison with the south coast of the mainland. The 'gangs' were usually very small, centred on a few well-known families such as the Wheelers, Cottons and Conways, but there was one impressive exception. Daniel Boyce (also known as David Boyes) of Alverstoke Bay, made an estimated £40,000 from smuggling by the 1720s. A blacksmith by trade, he worked profitable runs to the Cherbourg peninsula with his partner-in-crime, John Hatch, who lived at Stokes Bay, Gosport. Boyce's fortune enabled him to build a large house in Appley near Ryde (today a convent) where, in cellars which still exist, he stored a vast contraband cargo of wine. That Boyce was the 'Mr Big' of Island smuggling cannot be doubted. His team of smugglers was organized and professional and were rehearsed with alibis should they be apprehended by the revenue cutters of the excisemen.

So impressive was Boyce in his corruption of juries that in 1730 the government of the Stanhopes brought in the Balloting Act by which jurymen were picked indiscriminately from a locked ballot box. Boyce ended his days in the notorious Fleet prison, with its Painted Ground and Bartholomew Fair, probably dying there in 1740. It was rather ironic that during his time there, the keeper (governor) was Thomas Bambridge, possibly the most corrupt holder of such a post in any prison in the country.

The novelist and magistrate Henry Fielding visited Boyce's house in 1754 and noted, with a grim satisfaction no doubt, that the expensive books the smuggler had bought in London were themselves a con. Boyce paid the bookseller an astonishing £500 and clearly had not had time to notice that many of the books were duplicates, but bound in leather with different titles!

The smuggling methods adopted around the Island's coasts were largely the same as elsewhere. 'The whole population here are smugglers,' wrote the poet Sidney Dobell, staying at Niton in 1860. He continued, 'everyone has an ostensible occupation, but nobody gets his money by it or cares to work in it. Here are fishermen who never fish, but always have pockets full of money; and farmers whose farming consists in ploughing the deep by night and whose daily time is spent standing like herons on lookout posts.' It is likely that Dobell spent some time in the Buddle Inn, a notorious haunt of both smugglers and excisemen (but never on the same night!). During renovation of the pub's fireplace, some years ago, parts of a human skeleton were found in the stonework. It is impossible to say whether this was a smuggler hiding from the excisemen or an exciseman hiding from the smugglers.

The smugglers crossed to France, either in large, open rowing boats or small wherries, the larger of which were armed with light cannon. James Buckett, who was operating such runs in the 1820s had a 20-foot wherry called *The Bet* which could be operated by sail or oars and even though he ran his contraband in to the 'back of the Wight', the treacherous stretch of coast between the Needles and Freshwater, moored the boat in Newtown. Enterprising locals would provide the cash in advance – so much per tub of brandy, for instance and in that sense, men like Buckett were operating a sort of joint stock venture. The boat – and the risks – were Buckett's, but he took no chances when buying the goods in Cherbourg. Operating on 'the darks', the six nights surrounding a new

A table tomb in the churchyard of St Andrew's, Chale, traditionally one of the many 'hides' used by eighteenth-century smugglers to stash their contraband. Carol Trow

moon and knowing the currents and winds like the back of his hand, Buckett brought in the contraband at a pre-arranged point below Brighstone and Atherfield. Men waiting on the low cliffs signalled the all-clear by means of spout lanterns, which threw a beam of light in one direction only, to make detection by the land-based excisemen difficult. Such lanterns folded flat and could be carried easily in the inside pocket of the long, loose coats of the time. Alternatively, a 'flink' pistol fired an early kind of flare.

Once tubs were unloaded, Buckett and his one or two-man crew sailed *The Bet* around Freshwater for the harbour at Newtown. On land, men like William 'Bung' Russell hauled the barrels onto their shoulders and scattered to find their 'hides'. A grown man could carry four tubs, with the ropes across his shoulders and 'hides' around Sutton and Thorncross, Moortown and Mead Lane included convenient spaces in chimney walls and rafters, copses and woods and even table-topped tombstones in churchyards. Part of local smuggling folklore was the Niton tale of a gang led by a smuggler called Mussell. They were chased by excisemen and forced to hide not only their freetrade, but themselves in such tombs. Waiting until daybreak, one of them slid back the heavy stone 'lid' of the tomb to be confronted by a local lad on his way to the fields for his day's work. The smuggler asked him the time of day and the boy ran home, breathlessly telling his family 'Whatever wull become on us! The dead vokes in the churchyard be gitten out o' their graaves!' Since this story is published in a book about the Island dialect, it probably tells us more about how early nineteenth-century Islanders sounded than any actual event!

Calbourne, Mottistone, Rookley, Freshwater, Chale and Niton seem to have been the foci of the 'hides', but there is good evidence to support the existence of gangs operating out of Shalfleet, Brooke, Compton and Hamstead Ledge.

There were no doubt suitable caves along the coast at the back of the Wight so beloved of antiquarian and romantic novelists but these would have been well known to the excisemen and so became unusable and the fierce erosion of the last 200 years has destroyed them all.

From the 'hides', the next step was the redistribution of the brandy. The tell-tale tubs, with French identification stamps and bound with distinctive French rope, had to be burned and the contents transferred to other receptacles. This was usually the job of women, probably because the excisemen were reluctant to search them and it was relatively easy to hide small measures under an eighteenth-century skirt.

The Quay Arts Centre in Newport, one of the many converted warehouses along the River Medina, where smugglers and 'fences' stored contraband. Carol Trow

What if something went wrong? In the event of a smuggler running aground in treacherous seas, it was every man for himself. A horrified Methodist minister, John Dyson, wrote in 1865 of a wreck that occurred in October, three years earlier. The ship was shattered by the sheer force of water during the night, but the next day large numbers of people arrived, some to help, some to gawp morbidly, others to help themselves to the West Indiaman's supplies of drink. What appalled him most was the sight of so many Islanders lying dead drunk alongside the bodies of the actually dead seamen.

In the more likely event of a smuggler being observed hovering off the coast by an excise cutter, the task was to ditch the contraband quickly. To this end, ingenious devices were used to throw the tubs overboard with weights so that they sank quickly. Some had home-made buoyancy apparatus which meant that tubs could float feet below the water, invisible from the surface, but still attached to the ship. Since so many of the smugglers were fishermen, they had a story ready for the excisemen when they came on board. After the excitement had died down, the smugglers would return to the site with glass-bottomed 'peep' buckets, to see their tubs in clear water and grappling irons and ropes to haul them to the surface. Such a process was called 'creeping' or 'sweeping'.

James Buckett was eventually caught and pressed into the navy (a sentence for certain crimes, in theory, until 1951) after which he seems to have led an exemplary life. The three Conway brothers from Middleton operated successfully for years in the middle to late nineteenth century, long after the dreaded duties had been abolished.

What of the men paid to catch smugglers? Like all early law officers, the excise or revenue men of the Isle of Wight were undermanned and underpaid, expected to do the impossible for a pittance. In the 1750s, the officer in charge was the Collector of Custom, with his headquarters in West Cowes. Below him as a Deputy, merely, in fact, a book-keeper and twenty five other officers whose duties included searching and waiting, tidesmen and boatmen. By definition, the job of these men was to check the increasing amount of shipping sailing down the Medina to Newport Quay. Only four riding officers patrolled the Wight, one of them, James Blake, trotting along the coast in all weathers between Newtown and the Needles for £10 a year. The boatmen received £30 a year (about the same as a curate in the Church of England) but they had no powers of arrest and had to have the Collector in attendance for that to happen.

When Francis Arthur arrived from Kent to fill this post in August 1767, he insisted on his men being armed. The team was given two muskets, twelve pistols and six cutlasses. When he asked for a small cutter, a fast sailing ship that, at least had a chance of catching a smuggler, he was

Birmingham Hall - the house of Revenue Officer William Arnold in Cowes. Carol Trow

turned down however. Slowly, as the excise rowing boats became unfit for service, better vessels became available. At Yarmouth, a boat worth eleven guineas was provided and at St Helens, a £26 5s boat was built to replace the old one, worn out after ten years' work.

Despite the obvious disadvantages against which the excisemen worked, they did achieve limited results. Contraband discovered was sold off from the East Cowes Customs House and the proceeds went to the excisemen themselves, providing built-in perks and hopefully, limiting the risk of bribe-taking. The boats themselves were either burned or broken up so that they would be of no further use. The *William and Mary*, the *Launceston*, the *Wheel of Fortune* and *Miller's Maggot* all ended up in this way.

Inevitably the excisemen depended on information gleaned from disgruntled smugglers who may have had a score to settle with old mates. Isaac Peru was one of these and he ended up in Winchester gaol – 'a real object of pity'. Another was Thomas Mead who was ill-advised enough to become a revenue man himself. Continually threatened by his old associates, one of whom promised to cut his arm off, Mead was finally allowed to continue in the service elsewhere.

The eighteenth century was the age of the self-made man. While the government took no real interest in the causes of crime and merely, at the century's end, introduced ever more repressive measures under what has become known as the 'Bloody Code', individuals like the Fielding brothers in London began to make a difference with the creation of the Bow Street Runners. In the Island, the difference was made by William Arnold, father of Thomas, one of the great headmasters of the nineteenth century and grandfather of one of its finest poets. From 1777, Arnold, working from his house, Birmingham Hall in West Cowes, tackled the smuggling problem head on. He fitted out *The Swan*, a fast cutter capable of outrunning the nimblest smuggler. When she sank in a storm off the Needles, Arnold simply built a new one. The second *Swan* was a 90 ton, ten-gun cutter and the new Collector also had access to the 300 ton sloop *Orestes*, belonging to the navy. No smuggler in his right mind would risk tangling with her and her eighteen guns. One that did, lost her twenty six-pounder guns, 9 tons of tea and 2000 gallons of spirits.

The outbreak of war against Revolutionary France reduced the conventional freetrading habits of Islanders, but it also meant that Arnold's men had to be doubly vigilant to protect the island from spies. There is no doubt that William Pitt's government was paranoid about the risk of revolution in Britain and misread the signs. The vast majority of Englishmen were intensely loyal and followed Lord Nelson's dictum to 'hate a Frenchmen as you'd hate the devil'. Although no one this side of the Channel knew it, the French general Charles Dumouriez had already drawn up an elaborate and highly plausible plan to invade the Island in 1778. With landings in Sandown Bay, Chale, Brighstone and Freshwater, there is absolutely nothing the new Collector could have done, especially as most of the British army and navy were scattered throughout the world from Yorktown to Mysore.

Old-fashioned smuggling for old-fashioned purposes resumed after 1815. As promised by the late William Pitt, the government abolished income tax but was obliged therefore to increase indirect taxation – duties. In the first six months of 1818, 1200 tubs had been found in various 'hides' around the Island, twelve times the number thirteen years earlier. In February 1816 fifty-one casks of brandy were seized at Luccombe; a month later sixty-two at Shanklin; in December, eighty were found in St Lawrence. There seemed to be an epidemic breaking out.

With the death of Arnold and the increasing poverty of all parts of the country in the post-Waterloo period, a kind of resigned acceptance of

The Buddle Inn, Niton – haunt of smugglers and excisemen (but never on the same night!). Carol Trow

smuggling settled on the authorities. This is very evident in Commander Deare's report of 1836. As well as commenting on the huge involvement of the Island's population, estimating the probable smuggling rate of 10,000 tubs a year, he also laments what every Controller of Customs had been lamenting for nearly a century. He had sixty-eight men to guard a stretch of coastline (the Island's circumference) of seventy-six miles. Only fifty of these however were available for night work – essentially, the smugglers' time – and that consequently, the smugglers could operate whenever and wherever they liked. His evidence was that the cost per contraband tub was £1 cheaper in the Island than any other part of Hampshire. He had no right of search over individuals leaving the Island and could probably count himself lucky his men had caught sixteen people with illegal alcohol on them. He knew of at least fifty more who smuggled this way and had he no powers to stop them.

Even so, there were successes. The redistribution of spirits reaped the best rewards. Ann Dyer was arrested with a pint of brandy and eight 'skins' of Geneva (gin) under her skirt. Sarah Nesson was carrying two 'bladders' of brandy in her basket; the magistrate sentenced her to

The fireplace of the Buddle Inn. *During restorations, parts of a skeleton were found in the walls, but whether the remains of a smuggler or an exciseman will never be known.* Carol Trow

Winchester gaol. Proprieties could cause problems. One Bembridge fisherwoman took the opportunity of the wait for a female searcher on Ryde pier to relieve herself behind some huts. When she emerged she had changed shape considerably, but her 'bulk' lay under the water of the high tide. Children were obvious go-betweens. John Benzie, eleven, was caught on the same pier in December 1836 waiting for the packet to take him to Portsmouth. He was carrying six 'skins' of brandy in a basket and four of gin strapped to his body. He served six months in Winchester.

Actual violence between smugglers and excisemen was rare, but it did happen. Excisemen were protected under the Bloody Code; to shoot at one (whether he was hit or not) inviting the rope. There were one or two running battles at sea with the larger, armed cutters and still more cudgel fights on the beaches at the back of the Wight. Many of these stories seem apocryphal, like the exciseman stoned to death at Totland Bay; the revenue officers thrown off High Down to their deaths on the rocks below; the customs man who had his hands severed with a bill-hook when he refused to let go of a smuggler's boat. There are no names, no dates – just stories to frighten children in the long watches of an Island night.

There are however two tombstones in the Island which tell a real story. In what was possibly a case of mistaken identity, ferryman Thomas Sivell was shot and killed by officers in Portsmouth harbour. His grave in Binstead churchyard reads –

> To the memory of Tho' Sivell who was cruelly shot on board his sloop by some officers of the customs of the port of Portsmouth on the 13th June 1785 at the age of 64 years leaving a disconsolate widow and family.

The words continue:

> All you that pass, pray look and see
> How soon my life was took from me.
> They spill'd my blood which was so dear
> But God is good and just and true
> And will reward each one their due.

The very same verse exists on the tombstone of Richard Matthews at St Helens. Matthews was arrested with other smugglers on the beach at Sandown in November 1816. As it was cold, he asked if he could put his coat on. 'Touch it,' snarled the officer, 'and I'll shoot you like a dog.' Matthews ignored the warning and the pistol ball shattered his head.

The final couplet on Matthews' stone reads :

> And when you come my grave to see
> Prepare yourself to follow me.

Chapter 12

The Legend of Sophie Dawes

And never can we know what each one did,
For many a circumstance lies closely hid
Within the dim and yellowing files of time,
With many a dark and undiscovered crime.

'The Ballad of Sophie Dawes'
J R Brummell

Richard Daw was an oyster-fisherman living in St Helens, but his house on the green (which still stands) was paid for by his frequent runs to Cherbourg on the 'darks', all smugglers knew so well. His youngest daughter, probably born in 1792, was Sophie and her astonishing rags-to-riches story is not only unique in Island history, but is so bizarre that it has tended to be hijacked by novelists and poets. There is a blue plaque on the wall of her birthplace and the waxworks museum at Brading has a bare-breasted Sophie smiling enigmatically as the aged Duc de Condé, her long-time lover, twirls slowly at the end of a rope from his bedroom window.

How did a relatively poor man's daughter rise to become the toast of the French court? When 'Dickie' Daw died, probably before Sophie's eleventh birthday, the entire family – mother and nine siblings – had no

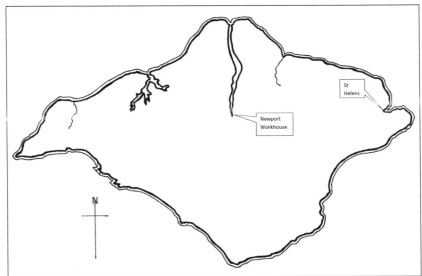

Location map 12. The author

The birthplace of Sophie Dawes on St Helens Green. Sophie's large family relied on winkle-picking and the odd bit of smuggling to survive. Carol Trow, with kind permission of the current owners

choice but to enter the workhouse. Her mother, Jane Callaway (from another smuggling family) probably never actually married the drunken Dickie. Her death certificate reads 'spinster'.

The workhouse had not yet achieved the shameful and sinister reputation it would acquire after the New Poor Law of 1834. Richard Worsley was enormously proud of the House of Industry and devoted five pages of his *History of the Isle of Wight* to it. The aim of the guardians of the poor, drawn from the ranks of Island gentry and the wealthier farmers, was to care for the old and infirm, but in the case of the Daw family, what was more relevant was the correction of the profligate and the education of children in the ways of God and hard work. It is almost certainly here that Sophie learned to read and write.

The workhouse must have been the biggest building the Daw family had ever entered, standing starkly on the edge of Parkhurst forest. Its dining room was 118 feet long, with large windows and whitewashed walls. It had schoolrooms, a bakehouse, scullery and an apothecary's shop, as well as workshops for spinning, weaving and shoe-making. The atmosphere of the whole place was designed to be uplifting and God-fearing, but it had its downside. There was no official uniform for the inmate paupers in the late eighteenth century, but girls there for 'persistent bastardy' wore yellow gowns. Prostitutes scrubbed floors (hence the term 'scrubber' that has persisted into our own times). Shortly before the Daws arrived, one prostitute was given two weeks solitary and had her hair cut off; two more were publicly whipped. By the 1830s when four prostitutes bound for transportation to Van Diemen's Land (now Tasmania) were returned to the workhouse for bad behaviour, Sophie had long gone.

Now literate, skilled up to a point in cookery, washing and scouring taught by older women like Ann Orchard, Sophie left her ordered regime of onion soup for breakfast and rice pudding and treacle on Saturdays to work at a local farm. Service of this kind did not appeal to the ambitious thirteen-year-old and she took the packet to Portsmouth where she found work as a chambermaid at the George Hotel. It may have been only weeks before she moved on again, drifting to London as thousands of children still do, believing some watered-down version of the Whittington tale, that the streets are paved with gold.

Sophie became a milliner's assistant, exactly where is unknown, but was sacked when her affair with a water-carrier became known. The date-line is hazy, but it must have been about 1807 by the time Sophie wound up in Covent Garden. This was theatre-land and girls in their teens (Sophie

The Baroness Fauchere, better known as Sophie Dawes from St Helens, from a painting of 1840. The author

would be about fifteen) earned their living selling refreshments to theatre crowds, taking part in choruses and seducing rich men.

One of these was an army officer living in Turnham Green and he installed the fresh-faced, powerfully built country girl in his home. Girls like Sophie were a commodity and relationships like this did not last long. When they parted, however, she received an annuity of £50 – never again would the workhouse winkle-picker be on the bread line.

Within weeks, however, Sophie was working as a chambermaid in a brothel in Piccadilly. The term was not a euphemism – brothels contain beds and somebody has to make them. Inevitably, however, Sophie, almost certainly by now spelling her surname Dawes, became one of the girls and had among her clients, Monsieur Guy.

The 'reign of terror' of the 1790s, an appalling outbreak of violence against the aristocracy and eventually *anybody* thought not to share the ideas of the Revolution, saw hundreds of émigrés scampering out of France in all directions. Many came to London, with tall tales of atrocities and determined to live, as far as possible, the lives of luxury they were used to back home. Guy was the valet of one of the most famous – Louis-Henri-Joseph, Duc de Bourbon.

The man cut a forlorn and melancholy figure. He was fifty-four, homesick and grieving for his son, the Duc de Enghien who had been assassinated on the orders of Napoleon Bonaparte in 1804. Sophie worked on him mercilessly.

Two other men were interested in her however, the Earl of Winchelsea and the Duke of Kent, father of the future Queen Victoria. The matter was settled over a game of cards, probably whist, in which Sophie was the prize. The Duc won.

By 1811, Bourbon had placed Sophie in a fashionable house in Gloucester Street, near Piccadilly and she sent for her mother to act as duenna-cum-housekeeper. The contrast could not have been more stark between the days of smuggling and scrabbling for winkles on Bembridge beach. But it was to get better. For the next three years, Sophie received a whirlwind version of the sophisticated education ladies of good families received from the cradle. She learned French (of course, bearing in mind her lover), Latin, Greek and music. She never quite lost her Island accent, but could pass muster as a lady of refinement. By 1812 she was living on an astonishing £800 a year from Bourbon and could afford servants of her own.

The rest of Sophie's life was tied up inextricably with the history of France. The overthrow of Bonaparte in 1814 saw the restoration of the Bourbon dynasty and the resettlement of Europe at the Congress of Vienna. Unlike many of the émigrés who had done nothing for years except wait for a miracle to topple the Corsican, Bourbon crossed to France, tried to raise the Vendee in revolution and was badly wounded in the left hand which left him crippled for life. When he returned to Paris in 1815, Sophie was waiting for him.

To be an exiled aristocrat's mistress in London was one thing. To be his concubine (still the legal and official term in French law) in Paris was another. Bourbon's father, the aged Prince de Condé, was still alive and the court of Louis XVIII was surprisingly stuffy and conventional. To cap it all, Bourbon had taken another English mistress, Mrs Harris, but the forceful and resourceful Sophie lost no time in removing her.

Between them, Bourbon and Sophie hatched a plan. She would remain his adoring mistress but would be married to a suitable husband so that her appearances at court could be explained; Sophie was introduced to all and sundry as Bourbon's love-child. The duped husband was an officer in the newly recreated Garde Royale, Adrien-Victor de Feuchères, who became Bourbon's ADC and was created a baron. The now titled Sophie married her dashing officer in London at the height of the 'season' in 1818, while all over England, people of her class were on the brink of starvation. Sophie's dowry from Bourbon was £5,600 – 269 times what an English labourer earned in a year.

1818 was also the year in which Bourbon inherited his father's title as Prince de Condé. His wealth was enormous and while Baron and Baronne de Feuchères lived in a wing of his chateau at Chantilly, Sophie also had access to his many other estates. She had a whale of a time, staging her own plays in which she played all the parts and spending her 'father's' and husband's money like water. Before long, servants and anybody else who resented the scheming machinations of the Englishwoman called her the 'Queen of Chantilly'. Above all, however, her double role in the Condé household allowed Sophie to be introduced at court. She had achieved the pinnacle of her ambition.

The peculiar ménage-a-trois could not last of course and it may have been Sophie herself in a burst of her increasing temper who blew the gaffe. Here, the accounts differ. Either Feuchères was the soul of dignity or he horse-whipped his wife. Perhaps it was both. Sophie was already making life increasingly difficult for Condé, humiliating him in public and taking a succession of lovers, including the old man's hairdresser. Trusted servants now worked for her, spying on Condé and reporting to her. Her mother and at least one sister lived in luxury in Paris and her nephew James, by now a meat-porter in London, was shipped across to become Condé's equerry and was given a title.

Feuchères' public response was impeccable. He resigned his commission as ADC and returned what was left of Sophie's dowry to the

Prince. He subsequently served with the army in Spain, but the final divorce from his wayward wife took seven years to achieve.

By 1822, news of the collapse of the Feuchères' marriage and the reasons for it reached the ears of the court. Immediately, Sophie was banned. She was hissed at and spat at in the street. Condé still protected her, but increasingly his behaviour was that of a childishly devoted, senile old man, utterly helpless in her wicked grasp – that, anyway, is how Paris and the court of Louis XVIII saw things. There were embarrassing rows, incidents in which Sophie was forcibly removed from the Tuilieries. Although no one in France knew her background, the winkle-picker's daughter from the Isle of Wight was proving a problem.

What drove Sophie now was a fervent wish to be reinstated at court – but how? Her plan seems to be extraordinarily complicated, adding to the enormous complexity of French politics at the time. Condé was by now well into his sixties and his health was failing. Sophie *might* be able to count on a sizeable handout in his will – after all, Condé had no legitimate children living. He did however have an illegitimate daughter after a brief fling with an opera dancer and the girl was married to the Comte de Rully. For a while, both women lived at Chantilly and the air must have been poisonous.

Sophie's plan was to persuade Condé to adopt the Duc d'Aumale as his godson and to leave the lion's share of his fortune to him. That, in turn, would make d'Aumale's family undyingly grateful to Sophie. This was no small task. d'Aumale was the youngest son of Louis-Philippe, the man who would be elected citizen king of the French in the years ahead and he was of the Orleans family. The Bourbons and the Orleans cordially detested each other, so Sophie had her work cut out.

The death of Louis XVIII did not see a rapprochement for Sophie. Louis's brother, the ultra-conservative Charles X, kept her at arm's length while so alienating sections of society that he was overthrown in the revolution of 1830. In terms of straight cash, however, Sophie was doing well. Condé had given her the estates of Bossy and Saint-Leu and legacies worth a million francs were promised to her.

With a mixture of threats, adoration and actual violence (Condé's servants often found him bruised and scratched) Sophie got what she wanted. On 30 August 1829, Condé signed a will granting everything to d'Aumale, except two million francs which went to the old man's 'faithful companion, Mme la Baronne de Feuchères.' She also obtained three more estates, furniture, carriages and horses and the ownership of the Ecouen estate, except that this was to be run as an orphanage for children of soldiers who had served with Condé.

On 7 February 1830, Sophie gained her final ambition and was again received at court, although King Charles was not particularly happy about it.

The 'July days' however saw the Bourbon king scurrying to England for safety and Louis Philippe became the new citizen-king, an uneasy mishmash of ideology that would stagger on, somehow, until 1848. d'Aumale was now dauphin, heir to the throne and in no need of Condé's fortune. The old man intended to change his will and when Sophie told Louis-Philippe, the instinctive reaction was the blunt – and for Condé fatal – 'stop him at all costs'.

During August, Condé seemed to be avoiding Sophie. On the 11th, she reached him and they must have had a screaming row because he appeared with a bleeding eye which he told a godson had been caused by hitting his head on some furniture. She caught him again on 26th, this time at the chateau of Saint-Leu and another row ensued. That night Condé retired late and was locked in his bedroom by a valet, Lecomte, a habit the old man had probably got into to escape the towering rages of his mistress.

The layout of Condé's private apartments was complex. All round him, in adjacent rooms and the floor below, were various hangers-on loyal to Sophie. The valet Lecomte fell into this category, as did her chaplain, the Abbé Briant and a couple called Dupré. The Prince's ADC, Lambot, was one of Sophie's lovers and her nephew James, now the Baron de Flaussans occupied the remaining room with his wife. Condé was effectively cut off from any independent help.

At eight o'clock on the morning of 27 August, Lecomte knocked on the Prince's door as usual. There was no answer and Sophie ordered the door to be forced. The last of the Condés was hanging from a window catch, a handkerchief knotted round his neck. The authorities were sent for and the word 'suicide' was used quickly and frequently.

From the Mayor of Saint-Leu and a magistrate from nearby Enghien we have a description of the body that tells a different story however. The Prince's body was suspended from two handkerchiefs tied together (nineteenth-century gentlemen's handkerchiefs were far larger than today) but the old man's feet were on the floor, his legs slightly bent. The 'noose' around his neck was so loose that the magistrate could work his fingers between it and the cold flesh. The face showed no signs of strangulation. Condé's face was pale, not flushed or blue. His eyes did not bulge, but were half closed. There was no protrusion of the tongue. When the body was laid on the bed and stripped, it was clear that Condé had bruising on his shoulders and legs, suggesting that he had been beaten or at least forced into position.

Because of Condé's exalted rank, a royal enquiry was carried out.

Pasquier, Louis Philippe's Chancellor, reported that no papers were found in the Prince's apartments; in other words, if there was a second will disinheriting Sophie, there was no sign of it now. The king's physicians carried out a post-mortem and Condé's own doctors were not permitted to attend. Their verdict, against all the evidence, was suicide.

Nothing about this makes sense. The bruising on the old man's body, the positioning of the knots and noose, the post mortem appearance of his face – all of it suggested, even in the pre-forensic world of 1830, plain, old-fashioned murder. Above all, the Prince's war wound, which had crippled his left arm, meant that he would have found it impossible to hang himself in this way. His bed had been made – hardly the concern of a terminally-upset man contemplating taking his own life.

If it was not suicide, what evidence is there that Sophie Dawes was involved in murder? The enquiry held under orders of the king, although carried out by officials, was not a trial. No one was charged; no one was under oath. Sophie's story was that she was summoned by Lecomte soon after eight and went up the main staircase to the locked room. Why, when she had a secret back way to Condé's bedroom? And why did Lecomte, who had a key, go to the lengths of this loud and public clamour? Because both of them needed the world to think that all was above board.

Sophie admitted to searching Condé's room for paperwork, helped by nephew James and the crawling toady, Abbé Briant. She explained this rather lamely by contending that she feared a second will would disinherit d'Aumale and make her sole beneficiary.

At some point during the investigation, the man leading it, Monsieur de la Hurpoie received a visit from the Procurer (France's equivalent of the Attorney-General) and retired to his country estate. By June, in the hands of carefully selected investigators, who later received appropriate promotion, the decision was that the Prince of Condé, seventy seven and crippled, had hanged himself while the balance of his mind was disturbed.

The following year, a French nobleman, the Prince de Rohan, sued Sophie for exerting pressure on Condé to make the first (and only surviving) will. He lost.

The court might have whitewashed the Baronne de Feuchères, but most of France did not. She and James Dawes left the country within months, selling off estates. James died soon afterwards, allegedly by poison and is buried in St Helens churchyard. The neglected tomb, with a baronial coat of arms at the top, reads 'To the Memory of James Dawes, Baron de Flassans, who died suddenly at Calais on landing from England on the 18th July 1831 in the 29th year of his age, leaving his widow, his family and friends to weep and lament their loss ... Erected as a mark of affection by his aunt, Madame La Baronne de Feuchères'.

The lavish tomb of James Dawes, nephew of the notorious Sophie, Baroness, courtesan and…murderess. Crow Trow

In 1837, Sophie bought an estate at Bure Homage, near Christchurch and a town house on the edge of Hyde Park. One of her nephews, Edward, was given an estate in the Island and the rest of Sophie's immense wealth was given to various convents and orphanages in France. The Baron de Feuchères was left £10,000 in Sophie's will, but he refused to accept a penny.

She died, fat and blowsy, of a heart attack in 1840, having developed dropsy a couple of years earlier.

To many Islanders, Sophie Dawes is a legend, a brilliant heroine who dragged herself out of the gutter into which she was born and reached dazzling, unbelievable heights. Of that there is no doubt, but she was also a liar, a bully and, ultimately, a murderess.

Chapter 13

'For Those in Peril...'

More than 4,000 wrecks have been charted by the Admiralty around the Isle of Wight, but this list is far from exhaustive and many have yet to be discovered. Even along the relatively peaceful north shore, tidal currents and sudden storms can be destructive; after all, it was near here that both the *Mary Rose* and the *Royal George* went down, whatever the specific reasons for their loss.

To the West, the fast currents known as Races drive ships out beyond the Needles and unwary captains have been driven aground on the sandbank of the Shingles.

The most dangerous stretch of shoreline is known as the back of the Wight. Its inhospitable cliffs, driving winds and sudden fogs made this a natural haven for smuggling, but it also is the graveyard of many a ship, shattered on the Brook and Brighstone Ledges.

To the south lies St Catherine's Race and beyond it St Catherine's Deep, where surging tides clash head on and make the area one of the most dangerous around the British coast.

Throughout the early Middle Ages, as we have seen, 'wreck of the sea' was an important part of the Island's economy and one of the men who made a great deal of money out of it was Walter de Godeton. Caught and

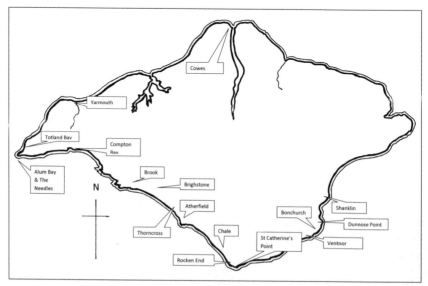

Location map 13. The author

The 'Pepperpot', the second oldest lighthouse in the country, high on St Catherine's Down. Its light, tended daily by a monk, ceased to shine with the Reformation. Carol Trow

St Catherine's lighthouse today - forty feet shorter than the original building - still signals a warning to sailors nearing the deadly Atherfield Ledge. Carol Trow

convicted, Godeton's crime reached the ears of Pope Clement V (in June 1314) and the Lord of Chale had an ecclesiastical court sentence added to the secular one. He was to build a lighthouse on the headland above Chale with a chantry and a priest to pray for the souls lost at sea. This was to survive in perpetuity and de Godeton's family were to pay for it for ever. The light, dedicated to St Catherine, and known locally as the pepperpot because of its shape (a thirty-five foot octagonal tower) is the second oldest surviving in Britain and was completed in 1328. It burned for 212 years until the Dissolution of the Monasteries effectively removed the monk who lit the fires.

We know the details of a few seventeenth-century ships that came to grief around the Island. The Dutch East Indiaman *Vliegende Draecke* (*Flying Dragon*) received a gash across her keel near Alum Bay in October 1627. Luckily for her two hundred strong crew, she was in the company of other convoy ships and they lowered boats to rescue them. The *Campen* went down the following year among the jagged rock formation of the Needles and a Dutch salver, Jacob the Diver, teamed up with Robert Newland, a Newport merchant to recover cannon, coin and lead, some of which was handed over to the authorities. The *Bird Phoenix* sank in Compton Bay in 1636 and the *St Anthony* went down in Scratchell's Bay sixty years later.

A combination of primitive navigation systems, careless pilots and appalling weather produced many wrecks in the eighteenth century and provided business for the island's longshoremen. This occupation is notoriously difficult to define. Most were fishermen or even farm labourers working land along the shore. In their spare time, at various periods in the past, they were probably smugglers or even pirates, but they also saved lives and it was from their ranks that the first coast guards and lifeboat crews were formed.

The log of James Wheeler of Blackgang, covering the years 1746 to 1808 is a fascinating record of wrecks and salvage, listing 110 wrecks and a whale. The loss of life could be appalling. On a single night in January 1754, five ships were destroyed and ten people drowned. All five crewmen of an Alderney cutter died when the ship went down off Brighstone in the winter of 1778. Six years later the *Earl of Cornwallis*, a man-of-war returning from the War of American Independence, went down off Rocken End with a hold full of stores.

The increasing number of wrecks led to masters and merchants petitioning Trinity House in 1781. The plan was to build three lighthouses to replace the defunct St Catherine's oratory; one at St Catherine's Down, alongside the 'pepperpot'; one at Hurst Castle covering the narrow western approaches to the Solent; and the third on the Needles. None of these was a success. Wrecks continued, especially below St Catherine's where the sudden sea-mists rolled inland and the light effectively disappeared.

Shipping increased in the Solent in the 1790s because of the war with Revolutionary France and the worst disaster in this period was the frigate HMS *Pommone* in 1811. She was carrying a rather bizarre cargo – Arab horses which were a present from the Shah of Persia to George III (sadly, the old man was by now too ill to appreciate them) and, more importantly, secret correspondence from Sardinia which was in the dispatch case of Sir Harford Jones, Persia's British Ambassador. In dense fog, the *Pommone* reached the Needles Channel on 11 October. It was tradition for the ship's Master to steer her at this point, but James Sturrock seems to have misjudged the narrow gap between the Needles and the Shingles and the hull crashed into Goose Rock. It was already dark before longshoremen arrived from Yarmouth and began unloading as much as they could, including the horses. The figurehead was draped in black cloth, a symbol of a doomed ship and Captain Robert Barrie remained at his post for three days until the evacuation was complete. 'The loss of the ship,' he wrote subsequently, 'is almost more than I can support,' but a court martial cleared him of any wrongdoing.

A similar narrow escape in terms of punishment occurred in the case of Lieutenant Durnford, employed by the Coastguard in July 1829. The *Carn Brae Castle*, bound for India but driven onto the rocks at Brook by freak weather on the 5th, was carrying stores for the East India Company as well as employees and their families. By desperately sawing down masts and hacking at rigging, Captain Barber was able to keep the ship afloat before the heavy swell broke her up. Durnford's efforts were unstinting but seven years later, he was clearly involved in smuggling during a beach skirmish at Totland Bay. A number of Islanders wrote letters of support because of the man's courage and tireless efforts in the wreck of the *Carn Brae*.

It was the wreck of the *Clarendon*, a 345 ton West Indiaman which led to renewed effort to improve the Island's light-houses. The ship had encountered bad weather all the way from the West Indies in October 1836, and it got worse as she neared the south coast of England. Apart from the crew led by thirty-four-year-old Captain Samuel Walker, there were a number of passengers on board, Captain and Mrs Shaw and their four daughters, Walter Pemberton a planter and his daughter from Nevis Island, West Indies, a man from Devon and a Miss Gourley from Portsmouth. The cargo consisted of arrowroot, coconuts, sugar, rum and turtles.

One eyewitness who told his story many years later was a Mr Holden who, as a boy, was one of many watching anxiously from the rain-lashed shore. It was 11 October and 'the sea was running mountains in the Bay'. *The Clarendon* 'was almost on her beam end and something likely to capsize as each sea [wave] struck her.' The crowd ran along the clifftops as the vicious winds carried the doomed ship along. It hit the rocks below Blackgang, Holden recalled and 'sounded like a box being stove in but hundreds of times louder [they heard the ghastly noise above the wind]. Father groaned and I started to sob.'

With astonishing bravery, ex-sailor John Wheeler lashed a rope around his waist and hurled himself into the breakers. With Holden's father and the others clinging to the loose rope-end, Wheeler grabbed a floating crewman and dragged him to safety. Then he went back for a second as the *Clarendon*'s masts crashed down feet from him. The fourth wave wrecked the ship, but Holden could still hear the screams of those on board – 'their terrified cries for help pierced our very souls'. Wheeler saved three men – the only survivors - and young Holden, soaked to the skin and in shock, clambered back up the cliff path to the ghastly sound of the ship's piano as the keys and chords broke – 'the awful clang! ... It was the Devil's music surely.'

The naked, mangled corpses were carried ashore after young Holden had gone, moving the people of Chale to tears. Captain Walker and his company were buried in the churchyard of St Andrew's, while the locals 'moved about like folk out of senses'.

Bizarrely, the only body not washed ashore was that of Miss Gourley. Her corpse, naked and swollen by the sea, rolled up on the shingle at Southsea, not a stone's throw from her family home.

The *White Mouse Hotel* behind the church was renamed *The Clarendon* in honour of the disaster – some of the local houses still incorporate roof beams made from her timbers.

By March 1840, a new lighthouse was in operation at St Catherine's. Built 72 feet above the sea, its tower was 107 feet tall, designed to shine out above all but the most determined sea mist.

Tragedies continued in the middle of the nineteenth century, despite the fact that this period saw the formation of coastguards and the beginning of what was effectively a life-boat service. 1822 saw the creation of the Coast Guards, an extension of the hated excisemen to control smuggling. Increasingly however, they were involved in sea rescue and their natural enemies, the longshoremen, began to work with them. So it was that the 'Smuggling Conways' were active participants in building the new Needles lighthouse, an astonishing feat of engineering completed in 1859. The light had to withstand ferocious winds and very high seas and her three-man crew could be cut off for weeks, hence the need for a fresh water tank

The slipway to the sea - the nineteenth-century lifeboat from Brook was launched from here into some of the roughest seas along the British coast. Carol Trow

and plenty of room for food supplies. The building was achieved by blasting the rocks with dynamite to provide a platform on which the tower could be erected.

The disasters of 1859 galvanized everyone into action. The vicars of Brook and Brighstone, two parishes in the back of the Wight, raised, with their committees, £600 in two months. The Royal National Lifeboat Institution could now afford to build two boats for inshore rescue. They were the *Rescue* out of Brighstone and the *Dauntless* from Brook, both 30 foot long, self-righting and unsinkable. They were hauled down to the water's edge by teams of horses and the launch, usually into horrific breakers, often at night and with a cacophony of noise, had to be timed to perfection. Missing the vital window of opportunity would result in the boat having to be relaunched, which could take an hour. A thirty-two pounder gun was used as a signal and the inhabitants of the respective villages were all involved in the rescue process.

In its very first rescue, the *Dauntless* lost a crewman. On New Year's Day 1861, in attempting a rescue from the schooner *John Wesley*, breaking up in Compton Bay, Coastguard McLeod fell from the crumbling cliff face. The irony was that the *Wesley*'s crew had already been taken off by a tug out of Southampton.

The first outing by the *Rescue*, on 2 April 1862 was to aid the barque *Cedarine*, marooned on Brighstone Ledge. Her 'cargo' was 191 convicts returning from serving their sentence in Bermuda; 134 of them where saved in the eight trips the *Rescue* made to the stricken ship. Unfortunately the whole event turned sour when the ex-convicts descended on the Brighstone pubs to celebrate their freedom and began fighting in the street. In the end, troops from Parkhurst Barracks had to be called to restore order.

By 1870, in what was increasingly an age of steam-driven ironclads with screw propellers, the Island had five life boat stations – Ryde, Bembridge and Totland being added to Brighstone and Brook. The appalling weather at the end of the decade produced an equally appalling disaster.

'One day,' wrote an eyewitness, 'when we were out on the cliffs near Ventnor, we saw a great splendid ship with all her sails set ... Then, all of a sudden there were black clouds and wind and the first drops of a storm and we just scrambled home without getting wet through. The next time I went out on those cliffs there was no splendid ship in full sail, but three black masts ... sticking up out of the water ... She had capsized in this very squall and gone to the bottom with three hundred soldiers on board. The divers went down to bring up the corpses. I was told – and it made a scar on my mind – that some ... had fainted with terror at seeing the fish eating the bodies ... I seem to have seen some of the corpses towed very slowly ashore by boats one sunny day. There were many people on the cliffs to watch and we all took off out hats in sorrow.'

The witness was the four-year-old Winston Churchill, spending time in the Island with his nanny, Mrs Everest, whose brother-in-law was a gaoler at Parkhurst prison. The ship was the *Eurydice*, a naval frigate used by the time of the disaster as a training ship, because she was a wooden-built three master and obsolete as a ship of the line. Two years earlier she had undergone a refit at the best known shipyard in Cowes, that of J White.

On the day that Churchill saw her, 22 March 1878, the Coastguard Station at Bonchurch noted her passing in its log and an artist, Ellen Sewell, sketched her. By shortly before four o'clock however, the huge black clouds heralding a freak snowstorm caused other ships in the area to run for shelter. The *Eurydice* did not.

Seventy miles away, in Windsor, three men were having tea when one of them, Sir John MacNiell, suddenly said, 'Good Heavens! Why don't they close the portholes and reef the sails?' The trio had not been discussing naval matters and MacNiell had no idea why he had said what he did, but he was describing the doomed *Eurydice* hitting that monstrous weather wholly unprepared.

Captain Marcus Hare, realizing the danger, ordered all hands on deck and a frantic hauling in of sail. The wind suddenly accelerated, changing direction and throwing the ship off course, forcing her over to starboard. As men dashed to do what they could, snow thicker than any of them had seen filled the sails and the sheer weight of it ripped off the mizzen and topgallant masts. The *Eurydice* suddenly straightened then nose-dived into the icy waters, pinning most of the crew below decks, such had been the speed of the storm. Those plunging about in the foam had no life-jackets and the astonishing cold paralyzed them quickly.

In an estimated 45 minutes, calm returned. By the time Mrs Everest had got young Winston home and made sure he wasn't wet, the sun was shining again and only wreckage and the mast-heads showed above the calm waters of the sea. Of the 366 men on board, only two, Benjamin Cuddiford and Sidney Fletcher were saved. They were treated in Ventnor Cottage Hospital (although of course there was no effective treatment for shock in those days) and photographed in the town's studio clutching what had saved their lives – Cuddiford a lifebuoy and Fletcher, who appears no more than sixteen-years old, a lifejacket.

The subsequent enquiries into the loss of the *Eurydice* exonerated the captain, officers and crew. The freak storm was just that and if *Eurydice* was rounding Dunnose Point, would have not seen the weather front until it was too late. Fletcher however had a different story to tell, to his family

A victim of Atherfield Ledge – the memorial to longshoreman Reuben Cooper in Brook Church, 1888. Carol Trow

years later. The *Eurydice* crewe was celebrating at the end of a three month voyage and were very merry – 'high as kites' Fletcher said – not, of course, expecting the sudden squall at the end of March.

The *Eurydice*'s bell still hangs in St Paul's church, Shanklin as a reminder of just how dangerous the sea can be. But no one has ever explained the odd vision seen by Sir John MacNiell nor the evasive action that had to be taken by submarine commander F Lipscombe in the 1930s to avoid a full-rigged ship that vanished before the disbelieving eyes of a startled crew.

The following decade saw fog, rather than storms, as the cause of most wrecks. The *Claremont*, the Essen, the *Cormorant* and the *Duke of Westminster*, were among the steamers colliding with the Island and the salvage work from them added immeasurably to the economy of locals, some legally, some not.

Modern navigation has meant that wrecks around the Isle of Wight are rare. Excluding ship losses that occurred in both World Wars, which are essentially acts of man rather than God, the hazardous work of the Royal National Lifeboat Service is arguably less hazardous than it was. One of that institution's most brilliant days, however, occurred on Sunday 31 January 1892, when a German luxury liner, the SS *Eider* got into difficulties in a thick fog on her way home to Bremen.

The *Eider* was carrying 227 passengers and a crew of 167, as well as large quantities of mail, gold and silver. Most people were enjoying a concert in the saloon at shortly before ten o'clock at night when the ship ran aground on Black Slopper, part of the deadly 'fingers' of Atherfield Ledge that jutted out to sea. There was no panic, largely because Captain Heinecke and his crew believed that the ebb tide would release the ship and all would be well.

Despite the jettisoning of some cargo – cotton and maize – the *Eider* remained firmly stuck. Eyewitnesses on the land recorded, as the fog lifted, what looked like a town on the beach, the blazing lights of the *Eider* illuminating the sea. The Atherfield boat, with Rufus Cotton as coxswain, rowed out to the stranded vessel, but the captain wanted tugs to pull him free instead.

Throughout the night the weather turned and the wind rose, the *Eider* jammed between two rocky outcrops and being buffeted by a rolling sea. Again, Cotton and his crew rowed out but Heinecke was still intent on waiting for the tugs, on their way from Southampton. By mid-morning they had arrived, but were in danger themselves of being shattered on the Ledge so Heinecke signalled the lifeboats for help. The *Catherine Swift* could not be launched in the rough seas so distress signals were sent to Brighstone and Brook and the *Worcester Cadet* under her coxswain James

James Cotton, coxswain of the lifeboat Worcester Cadet, *risked his life along the Bacl o' the Wight for many years.* The author

Cotton rowed out to get as many women and children off as the boat could carry. It took Brook's *William Slaney Lewis* five hours to reach the Eider, such were the seas and they too eventually rescued women and children.

When the wind began to drop by mid afternoon, all three boats hovered around the liner, ferrying passengers in a monumental eighteen trips. The passengers, drenched, frozen and badly shocked after their ordeal, were helped up the paths to safety, being taken in to warm fires by locals and given food provided free by Chale's only grocer.

By the next day the weather was even worse and most of the crew were still on board. Time and again it looked to watchers on the shore as if the *Catherine Swift* must be lost, swamped as she was by the huge seas crashing over her. After eleven trips, all hands had been saved and all cargo brought ashore. Over the next two days, forty-one more trips took place as, offered rewards, the longshoremen returned all £300,000 worth of bullion, handed over to coastguards on the beach. Did they all, perhaps, remember earlier times, when very little of that precious metal would have got back to its rightful owners?

The astonishing success of the *Eider* rescue made international headlines and the personal thanks of the German Kaiser. In the church of St Andrew, Chale, the Victorian memorial in gilt letters still stands:

Her Majesty the Queen commands that her warm appreciation of the gallant conduct displayed by the crews of the Atherfield, Brighstone and Brooke lifeboats, in saving the crew and passengers of the "Eider" be conveyed to them.

James Cotton received a silver medal for his efforts over those days, a fitting tribute to just one of a handful of brave men who risked their lives year in and year out for those in peril on the sea.

Chapter 14

'Nor Iron Bars a Cage...'

The Isle of Wight has suffered over the centuries in being part of the County of Southampton. Serious crime cases were heard in Winchester and this also applied to the Consistory or Bishop's court, which did not only deal with members of the church under the 'benefit of clergy' system (abolished 1827) but with laymen too. Island crimes tended to slip through the net a little as a result. For instance there is only one Island case which bordered on the criminal (although it was actually a civil suit) in the Consistory Court Depositions 1561-1602. Fifty-five-year-old Thomas Bedell, a butcher of St Cross near Newport was involved in selling the same piece of mutton twice in March 1585. Having sold half a sheep to Richard Lace, who would call back to collect it later, he then proceeded to slice off a leg for Margaret Reade. Not unnaturally, Lace was rather put out to find his purchase somewhat smaller than it had been and went to law. The outcome is not recorded.

Quarter sessions books for the Newport Borough Court exist from the seventeenth century. They were still partly written in Latin until the late 1720s and deal with the usual petty crime endemic in any town throughout the country. By the Easter and Michelmas Sessions of 1827, details are more forthcoming. Jurymen are listed, both for Grand and

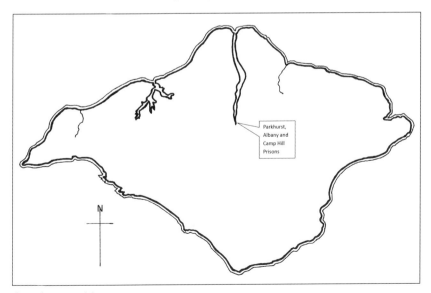

Location map 14. The author

To the Memory
OF
VALENTINE GRAY
The Little Sweep
Interred January the 5th
A.D. 1822
In the 10th Year
OF
His Age

An outraged public response to the murder of Valentine Gray, the 'Little Sweep': the memorial stands in Church Litton, Newport. Carol Trow

Petty Juries and the remit for these men was that they should 'hear and determine divers Felonies, Trespasses and other Misdeeds' within the Borough of Newport. Again, the information is limited, but at least we have names and specific crimes. John McGuire was not prosecuted having been charged with assault on William Dennett. Robert Osmond, on the other hand, was found guilty of assaulting Sarah Fuller and was fined 10 shillings. Benjamin Cooley spent fourteen days in gaol for assaulting David Chalk, a parish constable 'in pursuance of his duty'. William Pain was called to answer an unspecified complaint by his apprentice, Isaac Hawkins and it was found there was no case to answer.

The same could not be said of a case from the same period that does not feature in the Borough books. In the park at Church Litten, near one of the Medieval gates into Newport, stands a memorial. At the base are the words 'To the memory of Valentine Gray, the Little Sweep, Interred January the 5th 1822 in the 10th Year of his age. In testimony of the general feeling for suffering innocence, this monument is erected by public subscription.' Like Sophie Dawes (see Chapter 12) Gray is something of an Island celebrity, a new shopping centre built on the approximate site of his death.

Gray was a climbing boy, one of thousands of small children used by chimney sweeps to remove soot from the chimneys of houses, large and small. The job was highly dangerous and injuries and deaths were commonplace because of suffocation, burns, falls and testicular cancer caused by constant contact with the soot. When the crusading journalist Henry Mayhew visited a master sweep in London thirty years after Gray's death, he got the man to reminisce – 'I never got to stay stuck myself, but a many of them did ... and they were taken out dead. They were smothered for want of air and the fright ...' Many boys took their trousers off to prevent getting stuck – and that, of course, increased the risk of cancer.

In the case of Valentine Gray, he was so badly beaten by his master, Benjamin Davies, that the boy died. Public sympathy was outraged, but we have to see all this in context. It would be forty years before the National Society for the Prevention of Cruelty to Children was set up and sixty before men like Thomas Barnardo took up the cause of waifs and

This fireplace (in the author's home) was one of the last built before the climbing boys Act of 1867. It has steps inside and the flue is nine inches wide. Carol Trow

strays. Islanders like to believe that the tragic case of Valentine Gray, the little sweep, led to Charles Kingsley's allegorical Water Babies and that that, in turn, led to Lord Shaftesbury's Climbing Boys Act. If this is the case, it took over forty years for it all to come about.

In the Quarter Sessions book, there are frequent references to the Bridewell or Common Gaol which stood at the end of Holyrood Street and which may be what Sir John Oglander called the Cage. There are no pictures or plans of the building, but it was still listed on Ordnance Survey maps of the 1860s and must have been of a reasonable size to cope not only with the numbers involved, but the length of sentence.

The Common Gaol Book from 1838 to 1841 for instance, faithfully recorded in neat copperplate by keeper William Allen, refers to 256 inmates over the two and a half year period. The various categories include the age of the prisoner, whether and to what extent they were literate, the offence, any 'previous', how long they served and what their subsequent fate was (discharged to Winchester perhaps) and how much they cost in subsistence. All this should be a gold-mine of criminal information, but in fact it tells us very little. The categories merely refer to 'vagrancy', 'felony', 'misdemeanour' without an actual description of the crimes. The youngest case is that of nine year old William Bull, convicted of vagrancy (this, four years after the New Poor Law effectively criminalized poverty yet again). He was illiterate, had never been in trouble before and spent seven days in Newport Gaol for which his subsistence was 1s 9d.

Until the beginning of Victoria's reign, children were routinely sent to adult prisons, mixing with hardened criminals of every type, usually in large, open wards with no privacy at all. Recommendations of prison reform, from experts and philanthropists like John Howard, George Paul and Elizabeth Fry, had largely fallen on deaf ears until the 1820s when Home Secretary Robert Peel steered through the Gaols Act while simultaneously reducing the huge number of crimes that carried the death penalty under the 'Bloody Code'.

After four years of bi-party committee meetings, a bill was passed into law adapting the existing military barracks at Albany across the road from the Island's workhouse, to become a young offender's institution, 'where [such offenders] may be detained and corrected and may receive such instruction and be subject to such discipline as shall appear most conducive to their reformation and to the repression of crime.'...

The first intake, of eighteen boys, were removed from Millbank Prison in London on September 1838 and probably not before time. Three small girls, two aged ten and one seven were kept in solitary confinement for twelve months at Millbank before the scandal reached the Press and the regime was overhauled. Serious outbreaks of cholera swept through the

Penitentiary in the 1820s and there was generally a sigh of relief when the 'model' prison of Pentonville (which became the norm for all Victorian gaols) opened its gates in 1842. On the journey, the boys from Millbank stayed at the Royal Anchor pub in Liphook where they were fed well, but then chained to a wall.

Parkhurst was devided into two. The Upper Prison held boys of fifteen years and over; the lower, boys from six to fifteen. Until 1837 there was no compulsory registration of births, so the first intake might not have known exactly how old they were. This explains a certain vagueness of age in the Governor's Logbook analysed below.

The first intake went to the Probationary Ward, as all new arrivals did until 1863 into a block known as 'the corridor', a three storey building with 137 cells measuring 11 feet by seven. Each cell had a stool, table and writing desk. Because education was part of the regime, a Bible, prayer book and hymnal were provided, as well as a slate. The bed was a hammock, fifteen inches off the ground.

The daily routine followed the separate system which was now being introduced in adult prisons across the country. This even applied to religious services and the schoolroom, where wooden partitions screened prisoners off from each other. Two and a half hours of 'schooling' took place on alternate days only, with one and a half hours exercise (of the army drill type, since many of the gaolers were ex-military men) and half an hour's cleaning. The rest of the time was spent in the cell.

The older boys were taught arithmetic, writing and geography and their sessions ran to five hours. Various workshops were set up to give the boys a useful trade, including carpentry, bricklaying and shoe-making. The prison had its own allotments where the boys grew their own vegetables. Knitting was also taught, and each day a group of lads formed the 'pump party', lifting water from the 270 foot deep well to service the prison's needs.

Parkhurst's first governor was ex-Royal Artillery major Robert Woolcombe who selected his staff personally. His salary was £400 a year, as well as coal, candles and a rent-free house in the grounds which still stands. As he was still on half-pay from the army, Woolcombe could be said to be doing very nicely. The chaplain, Thomas England, who acted as schoolteacher and occasionally deputized for the governor, also had a rent-free house and a salary of £250 a year. The prison doctor, Benjamin Browning, however, received only £50 a year (less, as he pointed out in a complaint to the Home Office, than a cook) and he had to keep a pony and trap to visit the hospital each day from the house in Newport he had to pay for himself.

The *Illustrated London News* carried an engraving of a warder and two prisoners in those early days, the boys in smart shell-jackets, embroidered with the initials PP and a peaked cap with their prison number.

From the start, the arguments raged over the quality of life in Parkhurst, as in all prisons. There were those who referred to the place as an academy for young gentlemen, realizing that its wholesome daily food, clothing and accommodation was not only superior to conditions in the hulks, the rotting prison-ships at Spithead, but for the honest, hardworking lads outside the prison walls (see Valentine Gray). Mary Carpenter, daughter of a Unitarian Minister and founder of reformatories for girls, disapproved of prison for children because it failed to act as a deterrent – and judging by the 1844 Governor's Log, she was quite right. Today, we are appalled by the brutality of the Parkhurst disciplinary system, but placing it in context, twenty years earlier, the boys undergoing correction via whipping, the Black Hole or bread-and-water diet would have been hanged for their original crimes.

By 1844 the governor was an ex-captain of Light Infantry, George Hall. He was surprisingly humane, long-serving and introduced a system of wages for the boys which encouraged hard work. First class prisoners received 6d a week, second class threepence and third class nothing at all, providing for incentive. The 1844 log has five volumes and Volume 1 is typical, not only of the crimes and background of the Parkhurst boys, but of their behaviour while inside. Until 1853 transportation to Australia was the norm for young male offenders and of the 41 listed in Volume 1, 73% were shipped out on a variety of troopships bound for Port Philip: the rest were either sent to philanthropic institutions or, in two cases, pardoned. The youngest boy was eight; the oldest, seventeen; the average age was thirteen years four months. Twenty percent were first offenders; all others had 'previous'.

What else can the Log tell us? Where known, details were included of the family relationships of the boys and the description of the crime for which they had been imprisoned. A surprising number, bearing in mind most peoples' views of broken homes and crime today, are from families with both parents, the adults in virtually all cases employed, in some cases in quite well paid jobs. 60% of the boys themselves were labourers.

John Nelson was fifteen, with no occupation. He could read, but not write and was first imprisoned in 1842 for stealing shoes. Like all the others, he came from Millbank. His sentence was for transportation for seven years, which seems to be the standard for theft (the most common crime in the book). In the three years he remained at Parkhurst, he was punished ten times; for laughing and talking in chapel, quarrelling in hall during supper 'and exciting disorder'. He received two misconduct class punishments, eight solitary confinements in the Black Hole, a tiny windowless cell in the basement, and fifteen lashes with the cat. He embarked for Australia on 25 May 1847 on board the *Joseph Somes.*

James Simpson claimed to be thirteen, but was actually three years older. His father was a cooper from Lambeth and although James was a labourer, could read and write well. He worked with his father for two years, then ran away and 'got in with bad company'. Shortly before Christmas 1843, he was caught robbing a shop till and served two weeks in Brixton House of Correction. Back to his old ways, he was flogged and re-sentenced, eventually appearing at the Old Bailey for stealing silver plate from a house in the Wandsworth Road. Like Nelson, Simpson received ten punishments, but over two years. He showed disrespect to Warder Greig and was confined for forty-eight hours. He quarrelled in the bakehouse and hit a fellow prisoner, for which he received another forty-eight. He was placed in the Black Hole for laughing in the ranks and given ten days in the misconduct class for making a false charge against Warder Meerden. He embarked on the *Marion* on 17 September 1847.

The harshest sentences were given for arson – four boys all guilty of the same incident were sent to Parkhurst in the summer of 1844. Their fifteen-year transportation for what sounds like a boyish prank seems impossibly harsh by modern standards, but until 1822 arson, with all the awful unpredictability of fire, carried the death penalty.

Some boys behaved well. Fifteen-year-old William Hayward was presumably a First Class Prisoner. Sentenced to seven years transportation for stealing books in Birmingham, the former fender-presser was pardoned (why is not recorded) 'and sent to his friends' in January 1847. There was no misconduct while he was inside.

Two of the 'worst' offenders in 1844 were James Sturgess and John Keekin. Sturgess was a fourteen-year-old pot seller from Knutsford and came from a lawless family living in Macclesfield. An older brother was in Millbank and his hawker father had done time for 'ill-using his wife'. Sturgess had never attended a single day of school and ran away from the silk mill where he was first employed at the age of eleven. He was wandering the country with a gang when he was arrested for stealing five books (presumably to sell as he couldn't read). He received eleven punishments in as many months at Parkhurst, continually being disruptive after locking up time and using threatening language. He spent a total of five days in the Black Hole but seems to have escaped a flogging.

Keekin was a year older, a labourer from Newcastle-upon-Tyne. His father was a bricklayer, his mother a washerwoman and the couple had seven more children. Able to read, Keekin was apprenticed to a carpenter, but lost the job having 'fallen into bad company'. His first sentence came in 1843 for stealing silver from a shop and he signed on the coal-ship

Sarah Jane bound for St Petersburg (which must have made him the most widely travelled inmate in Parkhurst at the time). An accident on the ship however led to the loss of much of the use of his right hand. He was convicted of larceny, but actually received a pair of boots stolen by a friend. Over eighteen months at Parkhurst, he received forty-eight hours solitary for blowing a 'raspberry' marching from school. He found himself in the misconduct class for five days for using 'low and obscene language' and the Black Hole for 'murmuring at dinner table' (all meals were to be taken in total silence). On 30 May 1845 he was confined for forty-eight hours for 'filthy conduct' in his cell, which was the Victorian euphemism for masturbation. Such habits were widely believed to be the cause of insanity.

The boy who received most punishments was twelve-year-old George Carley. Sentenced to seven years transportation for the theft of four watches, the boy was the oldest of a family from Hull and had run away from two jobs as an errand boy. He was punished an astonishing sixteen times in two years and clearly had a bad temper and a mutinous nature. He constantly talked during drill, fought in the hall when he should have been picking oakum, refused to work and made a hole in his cell wall to chat to the lad next door. He received thirty-six 'stripes' and three days solitary for trying to create disorder in the supper hall and swearing while confined.

It is ironic that because institutions like Parkhurst kept records like this, we know far more about the lives of 'alien' miscreants than their local, honest contemporaries going about their daily business outside the walls.

'My wish' wrote the governor of Pentonville in November 1842, 'is that Pentonville will be for adults what Parkhurst is for Juvenile Offenders: a prison of instruction and probation rather than a gaol of oppressive punishment.'

Fourteen years later, all the good work of Governor Hall was swept away by arbitrary government changes. Adult males were admitted in 1856 and three years later, only a quarter were boys. The last of these left for Dartmoor by wagon on 1 April 1864 by which time Parkhurst was a prison for errant females. The change is well illustrated by the two royal visits to the prison. On Saturday 2 August 1845 Victoria, Albert and their entourage (Albert had recently bought the Osborne estate in the Island) arrived for an inspection. The boys' behaviour was exemplary and they sang the national anthem with such gusto that the Queen used one of her few remaining constitutional powers and pardoned two of the boys on the spot. The timing of the Queen's second visit was unfortunate. Large numbers of women had just arrived from Millbank and no regime had yet been set up. They refused to sing at all, cat-called to the royals from their cell windows and turned their backs on the queen herself. Victoria left early and gave instructions that no member of the royal family was ever again to visit a prison; that edict has never been overturned.

The new female superintendent, Sarah Wilson, was now faced with a mutinous situation. The women smashed furniture and windows and some of them got out into the exercise yard where they stripped off and covered themselves with tallow (animal fat). Governor Hall was asked to help but told Superintendent Wilson that her female staff had better handle it or would never get any order again. The female staff refused on the grounds that it was too dangerous, so Hall sent in the few remaining boys to turn the fire hoses on the women. Screaming and hysterical, they found themselves bundled bodily back to their cells by Deputy Governor George Shirlaw and his male colleagues. For the sake of propriety, married men only were ordered to take a blanket, cover the nearest rioter and lock her down. Governor Hall then went to each cell, calmly and quietly talking to the women until order was restored.

Within six years, the wheels of bureaucracy turned again and the women were loaded up and taken to a new prison at Woking. In their place came short-term adult males, with sentences of up to five years, but many of them were physically or mentally handicapped and Parkhurst had its hands full. The Gladstone Report of 1895 was designed to cope with some of this and a separate lunatic asylum for prisoners was built in nearby Nicholson Street. The warders carried staves with hollowed ends filled with lead, reminiscent of the 'life-preservers' carried by policemen and thugs alike. The asylum's log, compiled by the medical officer O F H Treadwell, lists a number of motives that sound bizarre. One man killed his child because the boy could not keep up with him during a walk. Another believed that not only was he himself a prison officer, but that he was also covered in green paint!

The irony of the Parkhurst story is that it is a microcosm of criminal life that is inevitably divorced from the Island. The prison officers who served at Parkhurst were drawn sometimes from the Island population and certainly lived in houses built nearby. But in no sense is the Parkhurst/Albany/Camp Hill complex a reflection of Island crime. That was going on elsewhere.

Chapter 15

Court News

arious newspapers have come and gone in the Island, but the longest survivor is the County Press, established in 1884. A trawl through the crimes recorded under what is today covered in a column called Court News gives a fascinating bird's eye view of crime in the community over a seventy-year period.

By the 1880s, Ryde, which had originally been two fishing villages, one on the muddy beach and the other further inland, had become the second largest town and its by now sandy beaches and elegant shops made it a fashionable tourist attraction. But there were still some no-go areas. Oakfield was virtually outside the jurisdiction of the Ryde police and was described as 'a very unsettled colony', inhabited by Italian organ-grinders 'and even less desirable characters'. The single patrolling constable had his work cut out, when the area at the top of St John's Street was often a battleground between rival gangs of youths from the town itself, and the outlying villages of Haylands, Binstead and Seaview.

Things were not much better in Newport. The Salvation Army, still only sixteen years old, had failed to get permission to play from the mayor and were heckled and jeered by the 'skeleton army' after complaints were made to police about the row the Salvationists made 'by seven sick people

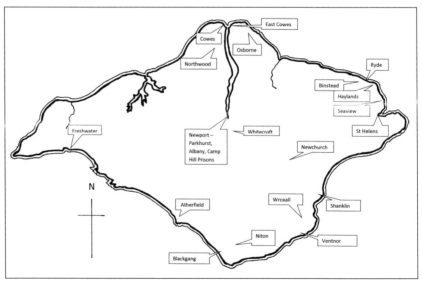

Location map 15. The author

and others that were dying'. In Ryde, the 'Sally' Army was covered in flour and soot by local youths, the lads being sentenced to seven days' hard labour with fines.

In Northwood in 1885, William Marshall was fined £2 9s by magistrates, not only for selling liquor out of hours (Gladstone's Licensing Act of 1872 was highly unpopular) but for attempting to bribe a police officer. When the constable showed no interest in £1 to turn a blind eye, Marshall offered him £5 – all to no avail.

Drunkenness was a serious concern to respectable Victorian society and the literature of the 1880s is full of temperance-style warnings on the demon drink. 'From many a [Newport] tavern at night,' a local reminisced years later, 'the sound of revelry arose while burly bearded policemen ... paced to and fro.' And in case the revellers turned ugly, the police had a handy picket from Albany barracks available to them.

Old crimes and old problems continued, despite the fact that Britain was now the most powerful country on earth, with an empire unrivalled in history. The *Cormorant* was wrecked off Atherfield in 1886 and the following year Reuben Edwards pleaded guilty to being in possession of two hundred weight of paraffin wax after his apprehension by the Coastguards at Blackgang. He was fined one shilling with nine shillings costs and had to repay the cost of the wax (28 shillings). Charles Chicks, his associate, was fined £1 3s 4d for receiving the wax and must have been particularly pleased when he tried to make candles that would not burn!

New crimes appeared too. David Block, a Polish Jew (surely a rarity in the Isle of Wight) was charged under the Vagrancy Act and discharged with a caution for offering indecent photographs at Ventnor.

Children throwing stones were a constant problem. Alfred Kemp of Gurnard was fined half a crown with seven days hard labour as it was his first offence. Another unnamed boy whose stone smashed a tram window that resulted in a passenger's cut eye, received six strokes of the birch.

In the year that the Whitechapel murderer was striking terror into the heart of the East End, polite sensibility in the Island was horrified at the bad behaviour on Ventnor pier. A Mr Cogger in particular found it 'very degrading to the town that dancing should be permitted there.' He had heard 'several complaints of the vulgarity and other things that were permitted ...'

Elizabeth Pragnell, alias Widow James, of Newport was charged under the Vagrancy Act with obtaining money under false pretences claiming that her daughter was in a London eye hospital and could not afford the train fare to the Island. She was given one month's hard labour.

There were interesting goings on at Wroxall where the unfortunately named Mr Bulley, the headmaster, was dismissed because he was too old, too deaf and his teaching was of a low standard, all of which would have the human rights lobby up in arms today. Less defensible perhaps was the fact that one of the Newchurch School Board was 'tampering' with one of Bulley's staff!

Parkhurst prison experienced something of a lull in these years. Now that the boys and women had gone, it ceased to be of much interest to reformers and did not make national news. The attitude of the locals however is clear from a newspaper article of 1890 when the Board of Guardians refused to allow convicts admission to the Workhouse on the grounds that there were already enough undesirables in the Isle of Wight!

Rather more humanity is evident in a bizarre case two years later. James Lawrence of Orchard Street, Newport, died of gangrene. A verdict of death by natural causes was delivered at the inquest even though his widow did not report the death and kept one of his feet, that she said had fallen off, in a sideboard drawer. 'Any other verdict,' said the coroner, 'might hurt the feelings of relatives and would do no good.' The same year a servant at Osborne (whether this was the royal household is not recorded) committed suicide by drinking ammonia.

And there was trouble on the ferries. Travellers returning from a day-trip to Cherbourg were asked to pay extra because the paddle-steamer *Windsor Castle* was obliged to put in to Ryde rather than its intended destination, Ventnor. When the passengers threatened to throw the captain overboard, he retaliated by threatening to clap one of them in irons, in the end using force to get them off the boat.

Island teachers were already facing criticism by 1893. The hands of a Branstone girl still showed scars three weeks after the caning she received from a teacher who complained that Island children were lazy and would not do their sums. The school pointed out that no written complaints had been received, but reformers retorted with the fact that that was because so few parents could write. At Newchurch, the School Board refused to provide shin guards to a teacher whose charges had been encouraged by their parents to kick him.

Blacksmith William Matthews carried out an assault on Louisa 'Dolly' Mole, a teacher's wife, who was an appalling gossip. The incident happened one July night as the Moles were returning from watching the fleet review from Ryde Sands. Matthews' claim that he merely intended to frighten Mrs Mole, as well as glowing testimonials from his employer and the vicar, led to a reduced sentence.

Another bizarre death occurred in 1895 when an unnamed, unemployed joiner from Northwood blew the top of his head off with a rifle. The bullet crashed through the ceiling and the floorboards of the room above, nearly killing the man's eighteen-year-old son asleep in bed.

Neither were the police exempt. James Duke, the ex-Deputy Chief Constable, was sentenced to six weeks hard labour after damaging trees in Hope Road, Shanklin. They belonged to his former boss, the Chief Constable and the state of Duke's mind was said to be 'uncertain'.

Escapes from the Parkhurst prison complex always made headlines. At midnight on 2 December 1895, John Morgan, serving ten years for burglary, made his way over the wall. He was recaptured the next day in a boat off Cowes, wearing the collar of a vicar. Three years later, Hugh O'Connor also got out and was also recaptured after an exciting chase involving one Ada Stark, a milkmaid from Dodnor.

Murder was already becoming rare in the Island when, in September 1898, forty two year old Maurice Holbrook of Freshwater walked into Newport police station and confessed to the killing of ten year old Percy Hayter of Worsley Road in the town. The boy's body was found in a field near the Albany Barracks and huge crowds gathered outside the courthouse to see the 'wretched man'. The motive was probably sexual, but in the event Holbrook was certified insane and ordered to be detained in a criminal lunatic asylum.

Another tragic death occurred in the same year but in very different circumstances. In the 'cup final' between Ryde and Sandown in March, Jones, Ryde's outside right, died having been hit in the chest by the goalkeeper's knee as he scored. The cause of death was given as 'two broken ribs and concussion of the heart.'

A vast change occurred in all aspects of Island life in January 1901 with the death of Queen Victoria. Ever since the royal couple had taken the Osborne estate as their summer retreat, anybody who was anybody in Victorian society had descended on the place. Poets Tennyson and Swinburne lived here; Lord Cardigan of the Light Brigade had two houses in the Island; even Karl Marx visited. But now, all that would change. As the spotlight died, and the royal influence spread to Sandringham, Windsor and Buckingham Palace, the Isle of Wight became a backwater, no longer the home of 'gentility' but yet another casualty in the public's insatiable demand for 'getting away from it all' holidays.

Violence however never quite went away. In what may have been a Mafia-linked 'contract' killing, an Italian organ-grinder named Rea from Oakfield was shot dead by a fellow Italian who fled to the continent and was never caught. In a tragic scene of the type which still commands headlines nationally, Samuel Hughes of Somerset Road, Ryde, cut the throats of his wife and child and then cut his own. No explanation is given in the newspaper.

And in case the twentieth century thought it had seen the last of old crimes - 'The scenes on Sunday [at Niton, after the sinking of a French brig, the *Russie*] will not readily be forgotten.' The ship carried thousands of gallons of cognac, claret and cider and 'casks and cases had been hidden away under the shingle and their tops covered with rocks and boulders. Undesirables flocked from miles around and were soon rendered drunk by the potent spirits. Some lay about in a drunken state all day while others fought and quarrelled. The scenes were described as like Bacchalian [sic] Orgies.'

And drink was the downfall of Alfred Wright on Christmas Day 1903. He was arrested for being drunk and disorderly and explained to the magistrate that he was 'fighting a lamp-post' at the time.

Football hooliganism made its presence felt the next year when referee Mr Spanner was chased from the pitch at the East Cowes ground. Supporters of Ryde's Sherwood Foresters verbally abused him, shouting 'unflattering sentiments' as they chased him as far as the floating bridge to Cowes.

The first motoring offence recorded in the Island was drink-related. Charles Edgar, twenty-seven, of Preston Place, Ryde, was fined £1 and lost his licence for three months for driving his car (make unrecorded) up Ryde's High Street in a 'reckless and furious' manner.

Neglect of children was as commonplace here as it was everywhere else in the county. In 1908, a woman from South Street in Cowes was prosecuted by the NSPCC for the state of her six children. They were covered in vermin and the matron of the nearby Mission Hall gave evidence that she had often fed them at her own expense and had to open doors and windows after they had gone to remove the ghastly stench. Their mother was said to be a woman of 'low morals', often seen in various Cowes pubs late at night. She got three months hard labour.

A peculiar case was reported later that year, again involving Ryde's Italian ghetto. Giuseppe Valvona, claiming he could not speak English, had nevertheless threatened to blow up a policeman with a bomb. The early years of the twentieth century were rife with anarchist terrorism and political assassinations, but Valvona seems to have been under the influence when he uttered the threat. 'I was not very much drunk,' he told the magistrates, 'only little much drunk' and was fined 1 shilling with 9 shillings costs.

More aware of the need for public good behaviour than we are today, magistrates set fines of half a crown to five shillings on Charles Lock, Jacob Honeybun and Ernest Vaughan for using bad language in a Newport street. It was probably already clear that punishment like this was not much of a deterrent; between them, these three notched up forty nine previous misdemeanours.

Among the Island's recidivists in 1910 was William Richards aka

William Durrant aka 'Tricky Billy'. He was fined 5 shillings with 7/6d costs for using obscene language, but his 19 'previous' included assaulting police officers, cruelty to children, larceny and desertion from the navy.

And in the same year, sixteen-year-olds Elizabeth Hunnybun and Elsie Jefferies were imprisoned for one month having been convicted of robbing their ninety-year-old landlord of goods worth £1 18s.

By this time, Europe was ominously gearing up for war. In the mounting paranoia that preceded the assassination of Franz Ferdinand in far distant Sarajevo, two Germans, a Dutchman and an Englishman were arrested as spies near the forts at St Helen's and Freshwater. They were later released without charge.

In 1912, Camp Hill prison opened as an experimental centre for habitual criminals and the papers screamed the headlines 'Pampered prisoners revolt'. Prison officers had soup thrown in their faces and inmates went on a kind of rampage not seen in fifty years. After a weekend lull, violence recurred and culprits were removed from Parkhurst's lower prison for birchings. Warders drew their swords to restore order and twenty of the worst offenders were bundled off to Portland or Dartmoor prisons, manacled hand and foot in batches of five.

In the year that the Great War broke out, there was a move to ban hawkers and street musicians from performing on the Parade in Cowes and the floating bridge between July and August. One county council member asked, in what was then purely a matter-of-fact way, whether that included 'niggers'. The answer was yes, if they were causing an obstruction.

During the First World War, the Old Inn on Hunnyhill in Newport was strictly out of bounds to troops from the barracks, but not, apparently, to 'ladies of loose character'. Neither did it prevent landlord Fred Virgo from being fined ten shillings with four shillings costs for being drunk on his own premises. In this war, as in the next, hardship abounded for poor families; a woman from John Street, Newport, was imprisoned for three months for child neglect. As she had been prosecuted before, the fact that her husband was a prisoner of war in Germany cut little ice with the magistrate. The South Coast saw sporadic bombing raids by zeppelins during 1916 and there were numerous court cases involving people who refused to obey or 'forgot' about lighting regulations. Church bells were silenced and public clocks were muffled in the hours of darkness. By 1917, the Island was declared a prohibited area and tourism ground to a halt. Food rationing produced long queues for margarine and led to forty South Wight residents being prosecuted for stealing by finding as they helped themselves to war supplies washed up at Freshwater.

Perhaps the appalling casualty rate of the Great War caused more traumas than we usually recognize. In 1920 the body of a woman was washed up at Ryde. She had escaped from the new asylum at Whitecroft and had waded out to sea believing there was an entrance to the underworld there. And juvenile delinquency involving football was already a problem when five boys from the village of Barton were fined ten shillings for playing ball in the Royal Exchange on a Sunday. 'This behaviour,' said the magistrate, 'has to be stopped.' It was possibly these same boys who were found guilty the following year of breaking and entering Shepard Brothers stores in Newport and stealing soap. The oldest, Truck and Eldridge, were sent to Borstal and the next, Lee, to a reformatory school for five years.

The slightly odd Frank Elliot was discharged in 1922 after promising never to return to the Isle of Wight having used bad language in Bridge Street, Southampton. The fact that his offence did not actually take place in the Island seemed irrelevant; Elliot's excuse was that he was 'the best singer that travels the road'. He received no dole and had twenty-seven children to support. He was sixty-nine.

That was the year that Edward Conmy became something of a celebrity. Escaping from a prison stretch of ten years for robbery, he evaded the law for two weeks, finally being caught in an empty house in George Street, Ryde, having escaped initially using a ladder and a gas pipe. His journey back to Parkhurst by car was like a royal progress; crowds cheered him and one woman threw him a white rose. His punishment for escape, loss of remission, basic diet for six months and shackles to belt and ankles, was described in London newspapers as barbarous. The next year, Conmy tried to escape again, this time from a work party.

The first escape from Camp Hill was done with a certain amount of flair. William Mason somehow acquired the hat and coat of the prison chaplain and simply walked out of the grounds. He was on the run for three days before being caught at Duxmoor Farm. The prisons were again in the news in the '30s. There had been a serious riot in Dartmoor in 1932 and the tabloid nationals claimed (untruly) that three companies of the Oxford and Bucks Light Infantry were on standby at Parkhurst armed with sixteen machine guns. For the first time in that year, two Borstal boys from Camp Hill reached the mainland; getting off the Isle of Wight seems to have been far more difficult than getting out of gaol!

The People's War (1939-45) produced a raft of legislation that had the effect of criminalising whole sections of society. Apart from Mrs O'Grady (see Chapter 17) the papers were awash with cases of people who transgressed, either for failing to comply with black-out regulations or not carrying identity cards. As an historic note, the cave where Michal Morey was supposed to have hidden having killed his nephew, was blown up during wartime military exercises.

In the year after the war ended, with austerity being the keynote and rationing still in place, George Jackson was at large from Parkhurst for eleven days and carried out a string of robberies, one with violence at the Horseshoe pub, Northwood. An unnamed convict behaved no less dramatically the following year when he was found, exhausted and numb with cold, clinging to a buoy off Egypt Point in Cowes.

1948 was an embarrassing year for the prisons. Some warders were charged with trafficking, receiving and theft. There were numerous escapes both from working parties and from inside. One warder was dismissed for smuggling tobacco inside the walls.

By 1950, there was a national sense that the country's youth had gone to the bad. Psychiatrists like Frederic Wertham labelled the children of the war years as the most delinquent in history. Deprived of regular schooling and in many cases of father-figures because of conscription, the 'cosh-boy' was seen as a feral menace, to be followed in the years ahead by 'teddy boys', 'mods and rockers', 'greasers', 'punks' and a whole litany of teenaged ne'er-do-wells influenced by the 'pernicious' music of Rock 'n' Roll and easy sex and drugs. Fay Hewitt-Brown was nevertheless painting an idyllic picture of a world we have lost when she wrote of Ventnor in 1950 – 'There was much excitement when three escaped Borstal boys were seen in the area and two of them were caught in the Rex Cinema. The film, appropriately enough, that was being shown was *Panic in the Streets*'. And the never-never again land image is complete as she adds, 'Policemen at that time were always to be seen ... it seeming that one was around every corner.'

Chapter 16

'Dear Osborne'

t might seem odd to have the classic Thompson and Bywaters case revisited in a book on the Isle of Wight, but it was here that the bizarre murder story began ...

Superintendent Frederick Wensley, one of the 'big four' at Scotland Yard, took a call from the Met's K Division on Wednesday 4 October 1922. It was from Detective Inspector Francis Hall who gave Wensley the bare details of a bizarre event in Belgrave Road at the intersection with Endsleigh Gardens, Ilford, the previous night. A Mr and Mrs Thompson had been out to the Criterion Theatre in the West End and had just left Ilford Station. It was about half past twelve and Mr Thompson, just passing a darkened sidestreet, suddenly staggered and collapsed. Hysterical, Mrs Thompson attracted the attention of passersby and a doctor was called. The assumption was made at first that Percy Thompson had had some sort of seizure, because all the doctor could see in the dark was blood around the mouth. At the morgue, however, it was obvious that the man had been stabbed in the back.

Hall's immediate boss was Superintendent Arthur Neil, but the man was on holiday, so Wensley took over. At Hall's request, he drove in the

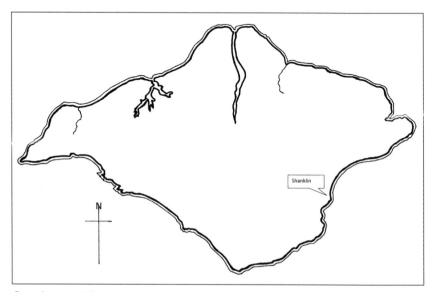

Location map 16. The author

pouring rain to Ilford police station, where a distraught Mrs Thompson was making little sense.

Wensley found Edith Thompson attractive rather than beautiful. She was intelligent, with an engaging personality and was well spoken. There would have been no police women at Ilford to sit in on the interview; 1922 was the year when the tiny female force in the Met was fully formed for the first time. But Fred Wensley was a copper of vast experience, stretching way back to the Ripper murders of 1888 and slowly, patiently, he got the details out of Edith Thompson.

Percy was a shipping clerk, thirty-two years old and Edith, a manageress and book-keeper in a milliner's, was twenty-eight. They had been married for seven years. During questioning, the seizure story had changed. Percy had been attacked by an unknown assailant who had run off down Seymour Gardens into the darkness. Wensley, vaguely aware of the shell-shock which haunted the survivors of the Western Front, pondered whether the attacker was mad – 'during that time,' he wrote, 'there had been a few cases of people doing extraordinary things.' There seemed to be no motive. Edith, still in her theatre clothes, was covered in her husband's blood because she had tried to hold him as he fell. She herself was not attacked and there had been no attempt at robbery.

Wensley talked to Edith's relatives and her brother mentioned 'a young fellow named Bywaters' who had been a lodger of the Thompsons. The brother was at a loss to explain how Percy put up with this man, who seemed to have been over-fond of Edith. There could be no connection with the attack however, as Bywaters was a ship's steward and was currently away at sea.

Returning to question Edith and another relative, Wensley noted a certain fencing going on and discovered that Bywaters was on leave and on the night of the murder, had visited Edith's sister, Avis, at her parents' house in Manor Park, less than two miles away. He had left there at eleven.

With his suspicions now thoroughly aroused, Wensley used the newly-created Flying Squad to track Bywaters down. In fact, he turned up at the Thompson parents' house again the next evening and was taken to the station. The eagle-eyed Wensley saw that the man's overcoat had blood spots on the cuffs. He found Bywaters, though only twenty, full of assurance to the point of arrogance and this was the wrong way to play an interview with a Superintendent of Scotland Yard who thinks you might be a murderer. There was no actual caution and Wensley continued with his usual avuncular approach. Even so, it was obvious that Bywaters resented the whole business.

He told Wensley that he and Mrs Thompson had been 'exceedingly good friends', they had exchanged a couple of letters and that Mr

Thompson seemed a little unhappy with this situation. On the day of the murder, he had gone to the West End in the afternoon, then called on Edith's parents in the evening, leaving at eleven. He had caught a train to Victoria, but missed the connecting one to Gipsy Hill, so he had walked home, arriving about three a.m. He had not heard of the murder until he saw the late edition *Standard* the next evening, had gone to the Thompson parents' house and was then brought by Wensley's people to the station.

In the meantime, Inspector Frank Page was busy searching Bywater's bedroom in Norwood and came across a bundle of letters which put the 'exceedingly good' friendship into perspective. They amounted to an incitement to murder.

'Yes, darlint [sic – an affectionate term used by Edith] you are jealous of him – but I want you to be – he has the right by law to all that you have the right to by nature and love – yes, darlint, be jealous, so much so that you will do something desperate...' All this of course was circumstantial. Wensley had a bed made up for Bywaters in the station library and Edith Thompson slept in the matron's room. The last thing Wensley wanted was for his main suspect to disappear on board ship.

Interviewed the next day, Edith was calmer. She admitted to the letters and their affectionate nature and those letters made it clear that she and Bywaters had had tea together on the day of the murder. Wensley had not told either of them the other was being held and when Edith saw Bywaters through a window, she suddenly cracked, screaming 'Oh, God! Oh, God, what can I do? Why did he do it? I did not want him to do it ... I must tell the truth.'

'The truth' this time was very different from the vague, fragmented memories of the attack. As the Thompsons reached Endsleigh Gardens, she now claimed, a man came out of nowhere and knocked Edith aside. When she recovered, she saw her husband scuffling with a man. It was Freddie Bywaters – she knew that from his blue overcoat and gray hat.

When Bywaters was told that they would both be charged with murder, he reacted angrily – almost certainly as Wensley hoped. He admitted jostling with Thompson, demanding that he leave his wife – 'He always seemed several degrees lower than a snake' – and that he had killed the man by accident, intending only to rough him up a little. Edith had just stood there, 'spellbound'.

Now that Bywaters and Thompson had been charged and were held in custody, Wensley and Hall could put the flesh on the bones of their case. More letters were found, in Bywaters' cabin on the P&O's *Morea* and, as Wensley admitted 'they played a great part in hanging Mrs Thompson'. In the midst of the chit-chat and endearments, it was quite clear that the stabbing was only the last in a number of murder attempts. After a 'Sunday morning escapade', Percy complained that his tea tasted bitter. His food must have tasted even odder when Edith put not merely ground glass, but light bulb shards in it, all to no avail. At one point, she ate the wrong porridge by mistake, but as digitalin was a cumulative poison, she reassured her 'Darlingest Boy' that she would be all right. The foxglove derivative takes several days to kill, causing nausea, bright green vomit, stupor and coma. Clearly, for an increasingly desperate Edith Thompson, all this could not happen soon enough.

Not only is this case famous for the legendary policeman who led it, but for the legendary pathologist involved too. In his day, Bernard Spilsbury had no rivals. A consummate professional and a workaholic, he carried out an autopsy on Percy Thompson whose body was exhumed by moonlight from Ilford Cemetery. No trace of poison was found.

The trial of Bywaters and Thompson at the Old Bailey opened on 6 December 1923. It was one of a handful that caused a sensation and there were queues around the block to obtain a seat in the gallery. It is also one where an illicit photograph was taken showing the pair in profile in the dock, both with tense concentration on their faces. The judge was Mr Justice Shearman and for the Prosecution, Sir Thomas Inskip (the Lord Chief Justice-to-be), Travers Humphreys (a distinguished judge in the years ahead) and Roland Oliver. A total of six barristers represented the pair, led by perhaps the most brilliant counsel of his generation, Sir Henry Curtis Bennett.

Bywaters effectively had no defence at all. He had made his admissions to Wensley and never wavered from that. Neither did he waver from his insistence that Edith was not involved. Curtis Bennett followed that line, explaining that the woman was a fantasist who wrote what she did to keep her lover happy and the various 'murderous' hints in the letters referred in fact to a suicide pact between her and Bywaters. On her own insistence, she appeared in the witness box and was torn to shreds by Inskip.

'I am convinced,' Curtis-Bennett said later, 'that Mrs Thompson would be alive today if she had taken my advice ... She was a vain woman and an obstinate one ... Her imagination was highly developed, but it failed to show her the mistakes she was making. I could have saved her.'

Bernard Spilsbury's reputation has recently taken a pounding. Today, we are less sure than his generation of the certainties of forensic science. Even so, in this case, his evidence – that he could detect no actual poison in Percy Thompson's body – was useless to defence and prosecution alike. It was, after all, a knife that killed the man, not digitalin.

The judge's summing up, on 11 December, may have been correct in law, but it was a lamentable lop-sided performance. Spilsbury, for example, was not even mentioned. Nor did Shearman remind the jury just how much of a fantasist Edith Thompson was. Typical of a man of his age and upbringing, Shearman was appalled by Edith's 'loose' ways. He was in fact trying her for adultery. The jury of eleven men and one woman retired for over two hours, then delivered their 'guilty' verdict on them both.

When asked if he had anything to say, Bywaters stood defiant and said, 'I say the verdict of the jury is wrong. Edith Thompson is not guilty. I am no murderer, I am no assassin.' Edith Thompson was far less stoical. Swaying and crying in the dock, she blurted, 'I am not guilty. Oh God, I am not guilty!'

Since 1907, it has been automatic for capital cases involving the death penalty to go to appeal. That duly happened under Lord Darling, the Lord Chief Justice and Mr Justice Salter and was duly dismissed. As often happens in cases like this, there was a huge wave of sympathy for Edith Thompson fanned by the Nationals, but the Home Secretary – 'the man who rations mercy' – would not be moved.

Despite the fact that it had been fifteen years since a woman had been hanged, the machinery of the law was inexorable. As the writer Rebecca West observed, Edith Thompson's greatest folly was that she had 'dreamed the wrong dreams ... bad dreams ... lead to lies and death.'

The hangman was John Ellis and he had a distaste for hanging women. Even so, since the executions were to take place simultaneously, at Pentonville and Holloway respectively, the Home Office requested Ellis at Holloway. Bizarrely, the hangman was given a choice of dates and Ellis chose 9 January (he was out with his whippets on the other date, the 5th). He received threatening letters – 'If you go and pull that lever and take a woman's life, Government ain't to answer for it. God'll send the bill to you.'

It was the first time any hangman had flown – the flight from Manchester to Croydon cost £2 5s – but he came back by train. On its return flight, in fact, the plane crashed, killing the pilot and two passengers. He was joined by assistants Robert Baxter and Thomas Phillips and together they went to Holloway.

The prison was in a state of full alert in case there should be a Sinn Fein (IRA) attack to rescue a prisoner who had been convicted for supplying arms to the cause. Ellis checked on Edith Thompson through the grille of her cell and turned away as the wardresses fastened her suspenders. For days the woman had been unable to do much for herself and had lost so much weight it was feared she could not manage the last walk. Ellis advised that a chair be placed near the 'drop' in case she fainted.

A small crowd of the anti-hanging lobby waited outside in the rain, a few of them kneeling in prayer.

At three minutes before nine, Ellis and his assistants took up their station. Edith Thompson was groaning in the condemned cell, having been screaming most of the night. No words of comfort from the chaplain, Glanville Murray, made any difference. Ellis thought she looked dead already, her head lolling on her chest. It was obvious that she was totally 'out of it' on brandy and officers held her on the trap doors while the hangman placed the pinions, hood and rope. He pulled the lever and Edith Thompson's body crashed into space, her neck snapping at the third vertebra.

This hanging came back to haunt John Ellis. The chaplain, appalled by what he'd seen, suffered a nervous breakdown and resigned. Others, like the governor, followed soon afterwards – it was clear that the tide had turned forever against the hanging of women. The two warders who had carried her to the drop spoke to an MP afterwards. He remembered 'their faces were not human ... they were like people from another world. Edith Thompson had disintegrated as a human being on her way to the gallows and yet somehow they had to get her there.' The haemorrhage she suffered on the drop may have been the result of a pregnancy, but nothing was found in the subsequent post-mortem.

At Pentonville, by contrast, all went smoothly. The executioner – William Willis – was usually assistant in hangings and his number two was Seth Mills. In his diary, Willis wrote, 'I told him, "Look at me and you'll be all right." He walked firmly, but not too quick. Death instant.'

Typically, Fred Wensley stood by his guns, whatever sentiment the execution of Edith Thompson evoked. 'This was a cruel and calculated murder,' he wrote, 'in which it was hard to see a redeeming feature.' Others agreed; the case was 'squalid and rather indecent,' 'essentially ... commonplace and unedifying...'

But let us go back, to the summer of 1921. Freddie Bywaters, then only nineteen, had recently moved in as a lodger to the Thompson home in Ilford. He had known Edith for years, when she was still Miss Grayson and the three of them, forming an increasingly tense ménage-a-trois, went to Shanklin, in the Isle of Wight, for a summer holiday. They stayed at the Osborne House Hotel along the sea-front; it is still there, although the name has changed. There is a photograph, probably taken by Bywaters, of the Thompsons that week. As Spilsbury's biographers wrote years later, 'Percy Thompson in a yachting cap, looks ... dour and uninteresting.' Edith however 'shows [us] this baffling and fascinating woman – for fascinating she will always be whether from pity or aversion – in one of her chameleon moods, looking her happiest, but quite unlike herself in any other portrait.'

That was because she had fallen in love. She and Bywaters had exchanged their first kiss, perhaps more, in that seaside hotel. If nothing else was conceived that week, one of the most infamous murder plots of the twentieth century may have been ... in the Isle of Wight.

Chapter 17

Fifth Column of One

'C areless talk costs lives.' 'Keep it under your hat.' 'Be like Dad – keep Mum.' 'Tittle-Tattle Lost the Battle.'

All these slogans and many more appeared everywhere in the Autumn of 1939 as a solemn Prime Minister, Neville Chamberlain, announced to an anxious nation that we were at war with Germany. Thousands of useless gas masks were issued to men, women and children. Thousands of cardboard coffins were made ready for a Blitz that took over a year to arrive.

The government became paranoid. Everyone believed there was a Fifth Column in our midst. Even the First Lord of the Admiralty, Winston Churchill, said so. And this 'malignancy' had to be excised once and for all.

One such victim of this excision was Dorothy Pamela O'Grady, a slightly dotty housewife from the Isle of Wight. She became notorious in the '40s as the only woman sentenced to hang for espionage in the Second World War. She had fallen foul of a complex series of legislation called Regulation 18B and Defence of the Realm Act. There was a hard core of Nazi sympathisers in wartime Britain, some genuinely impressed by the 'economic miracle' that Hitler had supposedly brought about in his ruined country and some openly anti-Semitic.

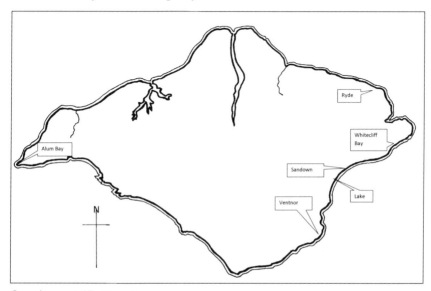

Location map 17. The author

Dorothy O'Grady, the only woman to be sentenced to death for espionage in the Second World War. The author

Dorothy O'Grady claimed that she was simply a fantasist, a sort of Baroness Munchausen whose tall tales landed her in the dock on a capital charge. 'Since I was a child,' she told the *Sunday Express* in March 1950, 'I have loved to make up tales and pretend I have done things that I have not done out of love of shocking people. At school I once wrote on pieces of paper that I had killed my mother ...'

What was in no doubt was that Dorothy had been arrested for soliciting in London and served time in a Borstal institution as a teenager for attempting to forge banknotes. By the year war broke out, she was running with her husband a boarding house called Osborne Villa in Sandown. Most of her guests left. Conscription meant that able-bodied men had to report to their nearest forces depot. The last thing on anyone's mind was a holiday and the Island, in common with everywhere else that had a beach, became virtually a no-go area. At times it was not possible to leave the Island and as the Battle of Britain was fought in the skies over the south coast and Portsmouth became a target for bombing raids, it was anything but a safe haven. Dorothy's husband, considerably older than she was, returned to London as a firefighter to 'do his bit' as was expected, despite the fact that he had officially retired. That left Dorothy alone with her black retriever Bob in an island full of soldiers, gun emplacements, a Radar station at Ventnor, on full alert against a potential invasion.

But prohibition signs, barbed wire and patrolling soldiers could not keep Dorothy and Bob off the beach. As Dorothy herself put it – 'I got to the beach at Whitecliff Bay ... I was sitting reading when two soldiers appeared. They asked me what I was doing there and then one of them ... noticed a small paper swastika pinned under the lapel of my coat.' In one of the least plausible excuses of all time, Dorothy claimed that the flag came from a *Daily Express* war map and it had somehow got entangled in her hair. The local CO interviewed Mrs O'Grady and informed Sandown Police Station. A subsequent visit saw a young constable ask Dorothy her views on Hitler. She told him the Fuhrer was a great man. Her home was later found to contain a number of other swastikas and detailed maps of island gun emplacements together with a false identity card.

In September 1940, Dorothy was apprehended by Lance Corporal Robert McAllister of the Northumberland Fusiliers cutting telephone wires to military installations. 'I had warned her twice before not to enter the zoned-off areas,' he told the Island's newspaper, the County Press in 1995. 'She offered me ten bob [50p but in real terms about £20 in today's money] to let her go. It was a lot of money as I was only on 14 bob a week, but I had no choice but to arrest her.'

Faced with a summons from Ryde Police Court, charged with being found in a prohibited place and attempting to bribe a soldier, she decamped to Alum Bay for three weeks before the authorities found her. The maps were serious evidence against her and Dorothy was remanded for three months in Holloway, being regularly interrogated by officers from MI5. She now claimed that the mysterious frogman from an enemy submarine to whom she passed her secret information was a figment of her imagination. In fact, given the high level of security in the Island in wartime, the arrival of a sub anywhere off the coast seems highly unlikely, but such was the paranoia of the time, no one was inclined to take chances.

Dorothy O'Grady's subsequent trial at the Hampshire Assizes in Winchester was held in camera because of the sensitive nature of the evidence. She was charged with nine offences under the Treachery Act and the Official Secrets Act which says as much about the strangulating bureaucracy of wartime as it does about Mrs O'Grady. Found guilty by the jury after an hour's deliberation on all but one of the charges, Mr Justice Macnaughten had the black cap placed over his wig and intoned, 'On evidence that admitted no doubt the jury have found you guilty of treachery. For that crime the law prescribes but one sentence and it is my duty to pass that sentence upon you.'

'The excitement of being tried for my life was intense,' Dorothy remarked later. 'The supreme moment came when an official stood behind the judge and put on his black cap for him ... the man didn't put it on straight. It went over one of the judge's eyes and it looked so funny that I was giggling inside and had a job not to laugh ... I found it disappointing that I was going to be hanged instead of shot.'

It was a commonly held belief that spies were routinely executed by firing squad. In fact only one of them was; the others died by the rope at the expert hands of Thomas or Albert Pierrepoint, the public executioners.

Mrs O'Grady appealed at the very last moment as had been the right of every condemned prisoner since 1907. Her solicitor, H R Palmer of Roach Pittis, forwarded the necessary paperwork and the conventional three judges, led by the Lord Chief Justice, Caldecote, duly heard the appeal, again in camera. Dorothy had refused to see her bewildered and innocent husband until this point but he was allowed to sit in court as Caldecote quashed the death sentence. 'It hurt me,' Dorothy told the Press later, 'that not once did any of them turn to look at me.' She was wearing a blue serge coat with a high fur collar and she answered her name in a quiet, strong voice. Even so, she spent the entire night after the death sentence was overturned crying hysterically. She was sent to Aylesbury gaol the next day.

Two years later Dorothy O'Grady wrote a full confession, which was passed to the Home Secretary, Herbert Morrison. It ended - 'I know I acted foolishly, but I did not realise the gravity of my acts at the time.' Her spell in prison was not harsh. Holloway had been given over to subversives of various kinds, but during her time, the 'regular' inmates were allowed back. She had her own sitting room, kitchen and small garden and her husband visited regularly.

In February 1950 she petitioned the Home Secretary – by now Labour's Chuter Ede – for release so that she could look after her seventy-two year old husband. It was granted and Dorothy O'Grady came back to the Island to re-open her boarding-house. She died in October 1985 having spent the last years of her life in warden-assisted flats at Porter Court in Lake.

Ten years later, there was a flurry of activity in connection with the Island spy. The then MP, Barry Field, was asked to investigate the case. Espionage cases heard in camera come under the thirty or hundred years rule and there was no Freedom of Information Act then to expedite matters. In the '60s, ex-naval intelligence officer Peter Hill interviewed Dorothy and made a documentary claiming that she was incapable of active espionage and was merely a delusionist whose silly claims were treated seriously. Hill had read the Directory of Public Prosecution files and was under no doubt that he was right. The files also claimed that O'Grady was arrested by soldiers of the Black Watch and not McAllister of the Fusiliers. Faced with this information, Mr McAllister, of Fir Tree Close, Shanklin, reiterated his story.

So what we are left with is two Dorothy O'Gradys. One is the miscreant with a criminal record of forgery and prostitution, with a fondness for Hitler and a habit of deliberately walking her dog in prohibited places, recording on maps the sensitive, classified information which would be of use to the enemy. This is the secretive, manipulative inmate of Porter Court who, according to the warden who remembered her, was devious and unpopular, only coming out of her room once a year for the Christmas party. Barry Field said of her, 'The evidence seems clearly to show she was recruited by the Third Reich at an early age and she never recanted. It is chilling to think that had it not been for the intelligence which led to her arrest, it would not be a Union Jack flying over Britain … but a swastika.'

The other version is the one acknowledged by experts like Peter Hill and most writers on wartime espionage, that what we should do is take Dorothy O'Grady's version of events at face value – 'I wanted people to think of me as a spy. I did all the things that were forbidden. I went on barred sections of beaches, wore paper swastika badges, made sketches of military objectives – and dropped them near sentries. Looking back, I realize I must have been suffering from a sort of kink. What I did in wartime was stupid and I brought the punishment on myself. I know people will always think of me as a spy, but I never was. I was just a silly woman who got the punishment she deserved.'

Chapter 18

'Look, Stranger, on this Island now...'

In today's media age, local newspapers act as a barometer of events, including those involving crime. In the past, beacons on lonely headlands warned of impending invasion; astonished Newport inhabitants tugged off their caps as King Charles I rode by; the Arreton church bell tolled for the funeral of murdered James Dove. Now, the Island's weekly *County Press* gives us a snapshot of crimes current, as opposed to the ghastliness gone by.

The edition of 24 October 2008 shows a procession in Newport to mark the start of the new legal year, as the Lord-Lieutenant, the High Sheriff, leading judges, policemen and church officials made their way from the new law courts in Quay Street, just yards from where pirates once had their warehouses of contraband, to St Thomas's Minster Church, where that great condoner of piracy, Edward Horsey, lies buried.

In twenty-seven pages of news, eighteen crimes are listed. The most common is of assault – four, of which three are drink-related. There are two cases of fraud (although one, still pending, can only be alleged); two of drugs offences; and one each of burglary, carrying an imitation weapon, harassment, animal cruelty, dangerous driving and racism.

Putting all this into an historical context is difficult. Arguably, the only crimes our ancestors would have recognized are burglary, fraud and assault. Everything else constitutes a 'new' crime. Animal welfare did not become an issue until the late nineteenth century, long after the formation of the RSPCA. Imitation weapons, which have been high profile in recent years, naturally, did not exist until a very few years ago. By definition, dangerous driving only came of age with the motor car and the recent electronic mania of speed cameras has criminalised the motorist – 'twenty' apparently, 'is plenty'. Racial comments were not illegal before 1976.

However we read these figures, what emerges is a safe place to live, one of the safest in the country. A recent crime report shows that 16.4% of Islanders binge drink, over 600 assault victims turned up for treatment at St Mary's Hospital and there were 18 class A drug arrests between April and August 2008. A safe place to live ...

Security past and present: the original watchbell, in Watchbell Lane, Newport, was tolled to warn the townsfolk of fire, invasion or civil disturbance. Today, the CCTV cameras record all of us, innocent and guilty alike, alongside the burglar alarm to local shops. Carol Trow

Camilla Petersen was fifteen. She was one of thirty-five Danish students enjoying a holiday in the Isle of Wight in the summer of 2002, a holiday organized by a Swedish company partially because the Isle of Wight was so safe ...

'She was a lovely girl, and a brilliant artist ... we loved her as soon as she came to us,' her host family told the County Press.

On Tuesday 16 July, Camilla shopped with a couple of students in Ryde in the afternoon. There was a beach party planned for that evening and with a little time on her hands, Camilla walked away from the King's Town of Brading where she was staying, the town where John Tyton had sought sanctuary in the church over seven hundred years before, having stabbed Nicholas Gentleyman to death. She went to sketch on Brading Down.

She was wearing blue jeans, a light pink T-shirt, a light blue cardigan and blue and white shoes. She carried a ruler, sketch pad and pencils, looking for a suitable scene to draw in the dappled sunshine in Kelly's Wood.

Richard Kemp caught the train from Brading Station, where the CCTV cameras showed a grainy image of the fifty-two-year-old carrying his red and black rucksack. What it could not show was what that rucksack contained – a girl's watch, a sketchpad, a ruler and unbeknown to him, a strand of brown hair, twenty five centimetres long. The Royal Naval Submarine Museum odd-job man caught the fast cat from Ryde to Portsmouth, then the little green-painted ferry to his home in Gosport. That night he wrote three letters, one to his aged parents and two to two couples, friends in the Salvation Army. He also wrote a confession to the police.

When Camilla hadn't turned up for the beach party, the party co-ordinator went looking for her. At 11.45 pm his torch beam flashed on a sight that few of us ever see and all of us dread. It was the naked body of a girl lying face down on a gentle slope on a quarry floor. Her light blue cardigan had been pulled tightly round her neck.

Thirty detectives and a team of SOCO parked on the windswept headland overlooking Brading and the area of Sandown Bay. It is a well-known beauty spot and viewpoint, a good place to park and watch the sun sparkle on the sea and the sweep of the Island spread out below. A cheery man sells ice-cream from his van to holidaymakers who cannot resist pulling in to admire the view.

They took photographs, swabs, carried out a fingertip search in the grass and leaves of 'Camilla's Place' as the scene is called today. The Home Office pathologist had told police that the cause of death was almost certainly asphyxiation and Detective Superintendent Alan Betts, head of South East Hampshire's serious crime unit was leading the enquiry.

That day, Richard Kemp was back in the Isle of Wight. He couldn't exactly remember where he went during that day, perhaps because it was supposed to be the last of his life. He carried his farewell letters and his confession in his rucksack and remembered lying naked on a hillside, trying to summon up courage to slash his wrists with a Stanley knife. He couldn't do it, so he swallowed an unknown number of paracetomol tablets and, his mind no doubt in a whirling torrent of emotions, called the police from a call box in Freshwater. The tape was later played in court:

'Hello, I want to turn myself in. I have killed someone. It was a young girl yesterday afternoon. I just killed her, you know. I strangled her.'

The police contacted Camilla's family, in the town of Holbaek, an hour's drive from Copenhagen. Traumatized, they flew to the Island and were taken to the mortuary in St Mary's Hospital, where Lonni Petersen formally identified her dead daughter. Then Alan Betts took her to Kelly's Wood because she wanted to see the place where Camilla had died.

For the first time in Island history, the police held a meeting with local council leaders and youth workers, largely to reassure them that, terrible though this tragedy was, it was a one-off and that the Island was still safe. A police spotter-plane flew all the hours of daylight, dog patrols were increased, shift patterns for uniform were changed and there was even more rapid deployment to 'hot-spots' where trouble sometimes flared between foreign students and locals. Existing liaison with student groups was stepped up. In the event, there was no panic.

At the inquest held two days after Richard Kemp was formally charged with Camilla Petersen's murder, and the head of the Island's CID, DI Clive Merrett, wanted to talk to three elderly ladies walking their dogs on the Down on the afternoon of the murder. After three days, the site was opened again and the fluttering police tape came down. Tributes appeared immediately. On one card was written, 'Such a peaceful place, such a tragic end, goodnight and God bless. Brading mourns.'

The Petersen family went home, issuing a statement: 'We will miss our lovely daughter terribly,' and asked that they should be left in peace to come to terms with what had happened.

The wheels of British justice grind slow. It was not until early November that Kemp appeared at Winchester Crown Court, not far from where another child-killer, Michal Morey, had appeared 267 years earlier. Both men pleaded not guilty. And both men were. The trial, opening in Winchester on 16 May 2003, lasted for four days. The judge was Richard Gibbs and the prosecution led by Jonathan Fuller QC. The jury, of eight men and four women, were shown photographs of the murder scene, with Camilla's body in situ and played the tape of Kemp's confession as well as his videoed confession in police custody. They were also able to read his 'last' letters.

What they did not know was that Kemp had a psychopathic disorder and a history of sexual assaults against children and had spent eight years in Broadmoor.

On the night of Camilla's murder, he had been due to go to a party too, hosted by the Salvation Army, of which he was a keen member, but he had rung a friend to cry off during the day as he had 'something to do'. That something was to cross to the Island and strip naked in Kelly's Wood. It was then that a Danish girl wandered up the footpath looking for a place to sketch.

'I took her by the arm,' he told police in the interview, 'and said "I have something to show you." She sort of resisted and I said "It's okay, I'm not going to hurt you."' But hurt her he did, strangling her with her cardigan.

Kemp's defence was one of manslaughter due to diminished responsibility, but the jury didn't buy it. After seventy five minutes, they returned a verdict of guilty of wilful murder.

'There is a striking and chilling feature of this case,' said the judge in his summing up, 'and that is the apparent clinical and total recall of what you did and why you did it ... with the evidence presented it is my view that it is most unlikely it will ever be safe to release you.'

'Camilla's Place' today remains as peaceful as it always was – has always been except for those terrifying, horrific moments late in the afternoon of 16 July 2002. There is a twelve foot high wooden memorial to Camilla, carved by noted Island sculptor Mark Sivell and taken from one of Camilla's drawings. It shows a warrior huntress, with bow and arrows, 'a guardian and protector of the woodland'. Two teddy-bears, sodden with rain lie at its feet and there are sprays of plastic flowers and a little carved wooden cat.

The Petersens often return to the island because they want to remember the place, not as somewhere horrible that took their daughter, but as 'a nice, happy place' where people come to have fun.

Since the 1950s, the role of the Island's prisons has changed dramatically. At first a Preventive Detention Centre with a relatively easy-going regime, from 1963 until 1994 Parkhurst had a Special Security Block for notorious prisoners. Among its first occupants were members of the Great Train Robbery gang whose hi-jacking of used notes on their way to pulping has passed into criminal folklore.

In the 1960s, there were discussions with the Home Office and Lord Louis Mountbatten, then Governor of the Island, to build a new top-security establishment (Mountbatten wanted the name Vectis to be used) but a dispersal system, scattering serious criminals all over the country, was created instead. There was a sense of unease in Parkhurst in the '60s (as there was in many prisons) and a petition was sent to the Home Office alleging the brutal misconduct of certain officers. It all erupted into a full-scale riot in 1969 when five officers were manhandled by over forty prisoners and threatened with a severe beating. Doors were barricaded and the rioters armed themselves with metal trays whose edges they sharpened. Order was restored, but only at the cost of injury to twenty-eight inmates and thirty-five officers. A subsequent hearing at Newport Special Assizes in 1970 cost the taxpayer £150,000.

That was the year that 'C' Wing was established, with its separate governor and staff, all volunteers, to house some of the most disruptive prisoners in the country. It was largely successful, with a small group of inmates getting almost one-to-one attention. There were rumours of drugs being administered however, like Depixol, known as 'liquid cosh' which kept dangerous men docile. All this came to an end when a rooftop IRA demonstration by Irish prisoners necessitated the evacuation of 'C' wing. It would not be restored until 1985.

It was ten years later, on 3 January, that everything changed for Parkhurst. Prior to that, it had a hard-man reputation, housing 'celebrity' lifers like the Krays, Denis Nilsen and Peter Sutcliffe, 'The Yorkshire Ripper'. But after the events of that night, it would all be different. In a carefully planned operation, Andrew Rodgers, Matthew Williams and Keith Rose waited in the darkness of the prison gym after the returning officer miscounted those going back to their cells. This was not actual carelessness – he was constantly interrupted during the process to make him lose count. They got into the workshop, put together a make-shift ladder from various improvised scraps and dropped over the wall. What they did not know was that they had a ninety minute window before their cells would be checked – and this, they proceeded to waste. One of the three had a private pilot's licence and they calmly used the call-box along Parkhurst Road to order a taxi to get them to Bembridge airport. Unfortunately, the plane they broke into had a flat battery and they scattered, hiding for seven days in the Ryde area. The national media followed the event and there were wild rumours of families being held hostage – two of the escapees were Category 'A', the most dangerous class and the third was a lifer. They were noticed hiding in a garden by an alert prison officer and the police picked up two of them straight away. The third got to the River Medina at Whippingham, but no further, after a police chase.

Heads rolled. The Governor was transferred, in a move that angered his officers and six members of staff were sent to other prisons. Within a year, Parkhurst lost its Category 'A' status and became a Category 'B' Training Prison, with the loss of ninety-six jobs.

Albany, the former barracks, is now a prison for sex offenders and Camp Hill is Category 'C'. As Brian Manser, a former prison officer and curator of the fascinating Parkhurst Prison museum wrote, 'If we recognize Parkhurst for the grand old lady she really is and accord her the dignity properly reserved for senior citizens, we should not reveal her full story but leave her with some of her private memories.'

As I put the finishing touches to this book, a new Chief Constable has just been appointed for Hampshire and the Isle of Wight. He intends to concentrate on three areas – providing an excellent police service, catching criminals and 'delivering an active police presence'.

To those who believe media scare stories about our feral youth, the disappearance of respect, the rise of drug crime and the case of the vanishing policeman, let me say – look back over the past of the Isle of Wight and be thankful we are in the here and now.

Bibliography

Bamford, Francis, Ed, *A Royalist's Notebook*, Oglander, Sir John, Constable, London, 1936 (Original publication c 1650).

Bathhurst, Bella, *The Wreckers*, Harper Collins, London 2005.

Brummell, J R, *The Ballad of Sophie Dawes*, Private Printing.

Cave, Diana, *Newtown*, Private Printing.

Dowling, RFW, *Smuggling on Wight Island*, Clarendon Press, Ventnor 1978.

Greening, Brian, *'Read All About It!' Sixty Years of News on the Isle of Wight*, County Press Publication, Newport, 2001.

Hockey, SF, *Insula Vecta*, Phillimore & Co, Chichester 1982.

Hooper, Paul, *Our Island in War and Commonwealth*, Cross Publications, Chale, 1998.

Hutchings, Richard, *Smugglers of the Isle of Wight*, GG Saunders, Shanklin 1972.

Jones, Jack & Johanna, *The Isle of Wight*, Dovecote Press, Wimbourne, 1987.

Jones, Jack, *The Royal Prisoner*, Lutterworth, London 1965.

Lawless, Naomi, *Newport*, Tempus, Stroud, 2002.

Manser, Brian, *Behind the Small Wooden Door*, Coach House Publications, Freshwater, 2000.

Medlund, J C, *The Making of the Wight*, Isle of Wight Beacon, Ltd, Newport, 2007.

Medlund, , J C, *Shipwrecks of the Wight*, West Island Printers, Freshwater 1986.

Phillips, Kenneth, *For Rooks and Ravens*, IOW Museums Publications, IOW 1982.

Phillips, Kenneth, *Shipwrecks of the Isle of Wight*, David and Charles, Newton Abbott, 1988.

Robbins, R Ed, *The History of the Isle of Wight*, Worsley, Sir Richard, EP Publishing, Wakefield, 1975 (Originally published 1781).

Rule, Margaret, *The Mary Rose*, Conway Maritime Press, London, 1982.

Ryde Social Heritage Group, *Ryde's Heritage; Our Town, Your Histories*, Ryde Social Heritage Group, Ryde, 2008.

Wensley, Supt Fred, *Forty Years of Scotland Yard*, Doubleday, London 1931.

Wilson, Lawrence, *Portrait of the Isle of Wight*, Robert Hale, London 1965.

Publications, Ephemera and Maps

Isle of Wight County Press – various dates.

Parkhurst Prison Governor's Log 1844.

Timeline Historical Map 1810-11 Ordnance Survey 196.

Transcript of the Trial of Captain George Bissett for Criminal Conversation with Lady Worsley 1782.

A History Military and Municipal of the Ancient Borough of the Devizes. James Waylan, 1859.

Index